Acclaim f

MW01591561

Planning For College

"Along with lots of original strategies to save you in college costs, this book is a welcome stress-reliever for parents who haven't a clue about how to get into college."

Dan Maga, CEO
American College Funding, Chicago, IL

"Forget your highlighter - every page is loaded with facts you can use right now! And it's fun to read."

Joe Eberle
The College Store, Denver, CO

"I love the brevity and depth of this book! You can save a bundle by opening this book to any page."

Ron Caruthers, College Professor & CEO
College Planning Specialists, Carlsbad, CA

"To win the college game, this is the playbook to use."

Curtis Smith
Chartered Financial Consultant, Charlestown, RI

"Paul Hemphill is my "go to" guy when it comes to planning for college...His no-frills approach to college planning places parents and students in the 'driver's seat'...that is not only the best fit for the student but the best financial fit for the parents."

Suzanne Shaffer
Parents Countdown To College Coach, Corpus Christi, TX

"A trove of information that you won't find anywhere else - honest, original, and developed over years of on-the-ground experience. An essential tool in any parent's college preparation arsenal."

Anthony-James Green, Founder
Test Prep Authority, New York, NY

"This is an excellent book...provides the hard TRUTH...regardless of how politically-correct that truth may or may not be. As a parent of four college-bound, Im so glad to have this book as a continual resource."

Celest Horton
Founder of How to Pay for College HQ, Phoenix, AZ

Also by Paul Lloyd Hemphill

Why You're Already A Leader
Gettysburg Lessons in the Digital Age

Planning For College

Easiest Ways To Get In
And Pay Less

Paul Lloyd Hemphill

First Edition: May, 2014
Second Edition: June, 2016

Library of Congress Control Number: 2016902572

ISBN-10:   0-9785482-6-4

ISBN-13: 978-0-9785482-6-1

1. College planning   2. College admission 3. College financial aid

Printed and bound in the United States of America
Published by One White's Pond Press
Norfolk, MA

Legal Notice

Table of Contents

Introduction

Open this book to any page. Valuable tips are everywhere.

Most helpful books on American colleges deal only with financial aid, and those that deal with college admissions are usually targeting the brightest kids on how to get into the highest profile schools. By contrast you get a double whammy here: with razor-cutting humor you get a solid read of the financial aid AND the admissions processes, regardless of income.

The powerful strategies found in this book make it easier to be admitted and to pay for college. Even the *Article Sources* in the back of this book has a whole lot of additional information you can use.

The author gives you a very realistic if not disturbing picture of what your money will buy. The author calls it a game that you must play by someone else's rules. It's one more reason why this book stands alone from other college how-to books.

For the years I've been working with the FAFSA and CSS Profile, college applications, resumes, and essays, this is the most practical beginner's book on the combined subjects of admissions and financial aid.

This little gem of a book couldn't have come at a better time.

Irene McGann
www.planningforcollege.net

Planning For College

Warning

This book introduces the game colleges play at the expense of both students and parents, and reveals the least-known and perfectly legal strategies to help parents win.

Colleges are well aware that parents don't know that college admissions and financial aid constitute a game that's played by *their* rules and on *their* playing fields. Perhaps college administrators think you're either too blind to see it, too busy to notice it, or too naïve to believe it. One thing is for sure: they're too arrogant to care.

Part of their arrogance comes from many of today's college presidents and professors who are children from the counter-cultural experiment of the 1960s. They wanted to change the world with non-stop street protests, energized by an adolescent moral relativism that said, "If it feels right, do it, and don't worry about the consequences."

Today they teach that there's no such thing as evil in the world, just misunderstandings of competing ideologies. Emblematic of their close-mindedness and dogmatism, they educate as if 9/11 never happened, demand that we appreciate radicals as victims who kill people over a cartoon depiction of Mohammed, and conveniently ignore that reenlistments of American soldiers of college age are at an all-time high.

Many of these intellectual punks never grew up, and parents are unknowingly feeding their children to these frustrated lions of indoctrination and drivel, who have taken their protests from the streets and into the classrooms. Moreover, there's a lopsided majority of professors who hold the same political beliefs, marked by intolerance for opposing opinions, who use their classrooms to preach instead of teach. True to form, they hire professors who are mirror-images of themselves.

To add insult to injury, many have tenure, which is a life-time job with a guaranteed paycheck, without the attendant guarantee of intellectual integrity or academic excellence. Law professor, Alan Dershowitz, observed that "...tenured professors at major universities...are among the biggest cowards. They use tenure as a sword..." Eighty-eight (88) professors at Duke University signed a statement condemning three students for rape. When the students were proven innocent, we're still waiting for just one of those professors to come forward with a signed letter of apology. As professors remain the Untouchables with no accountability for their words or actions, like it or not, parents are forced to pay their salaries.

As if to champion arrogance, the Ivy League schools act like privileged brats who bask in the heartbreak of the defeated. Instead of announcing every April the impressive profiles of the next freshmen class, they can't contain their excitement in telling the world of the high percentage of applicants they *reject*. Their hypocrisy matches their arrogance with claims of helping low-income students: in 2005 these schools managed to give full scholarships to a grand total of 46 poor students nationwide. Their shock-and-awe capacity to crush hopes and dreams and manufacture window-dressing is worn like badges of honor.

A virus surrounds the college game. It's called commercialization. A former Harvard president believes everything in a university is for sale at the right price. Profiting from big-time college sports and research for major corporations, core academic values are being undermined, and the disease of mediocrity remains virtually untreated. Most Roman Catholic colleges, where a single course in Catholic theology is no longer required to graduate, have surrendered their religious identity for adoration of the truly Almighty: the Dollar.

No longer do we have institutions of higher learning, but business enterprises where schools are brand names, departments are profit centers, professors are employees, parents are customers, students are consumers, and a degree is a receipt.

This book is not meant to explore this virus in depth nor does it pretend to offer antidotes. Yet it does provide a diagnosis in the form of stand-alone billboard statements from prominent critics of American higher education who are educators themselves. These insiders warn of the harm being done to the body of quality education of a generation ago.

Today the classic search for truth has been replaced by the ordinary expression of opinion, merit is mocked as students easily get A*s* and B*s* for only 10-15 hours of study per week, and lower-paid, part-time professors represent nearly half of all American faculties. Higher education is getting lower, which makes our colleges overpriced brain dumps for our children.

Feeling overwhelmed and inadequate as individuals to do anything to improve the nation's educational values, parents and students are reduced to playing a game that hammers them financially. Like a dreadful New England winter, they are helpless to change it, so they accept and deal with it in the cold comfort it will only last for four years.

The typical book on admissions and financial aid is similar to an excellent travel guide to a foreign land, but gives little indication that your destination is unfriendly territory, or that nearly every feature of your stay is dreadfully expensive. On the other hand, this book is the only one with a pre-travel advisory: it warns you of what your money is really purchasing before you leave on your journey.

The college game is already in full swing, and your financial comfort zone is headed for a huge upset. The college award letter finally arrives in late March, and you see what the school is giving your student each semester. Finally, you read the blunt reality: what you have to spend.

Nothing has the potential to wreak more havoc, or to do more damage to your retirement in so short a time than the college game. But the proven financial aid strategies found here are perfectly legal. The colleges hope that parents of college-bound students never discover the contents of this book. After all, they're in this game to win and win big. Yet they are very comfortable on their mountain of winnings to the point of indifference to the strategies presented here, or they do little or nothing to foil your attempts to use them. Not even the popularity of this book will change their thinking. Ironically, their arrogance will allow you to use the information in these pages to score often and win big.

Paul Lloyd Hemphill
Norfolk, MA

Other Words of Warning
Why You'll Pay Too Much

"Tuition is set high...and whatever else we think can be extracted from parents. In the last 10 years of committee meetings on [Boston University's] annual tuition adjustment, the only real question was, 'How much can we get away with?'"

Professor Peter Wood
"The Big Steal," National Review Online, 6/6/04

"The Chronicle of Higher Education recently released its own survey of university presidents, and its results confirm that... Five of the six most pressing issues have to do with money, and the sixth - retaining students - is only marginally related to teaching and learning."

John Merrow, "Where Are the Voices of College Presidents?"
Christian Science Monitor website, 12/21/05

"The signs of erosion on our campuses are undeniable....it remains obsessed with a racial, ideological, and sexual spoils system called 'diversity.'"

Victor Davis Hanson
Wall Street Journal, 9/27/2005

"Faculty expectations and standards have been lowered, more students come to college under-prepared, and grades have been inflated. Retention and graduation rates are considered more important than what is or is not being learned."

Richard H. Hersh
Former President, Trinity College (CT)

"Higher education is a business, and access must first preserve the institution's fiscal integrity."

Toward a Taxonomy of the Admissions Decision-Making Process
Graff, Perfetto, Escandon, Rigol and Schmidt, 1999

The End
What This Book Will Do For You

Your confusions, illusions and delusions about applying to college and how to pay for it are coming to an end. This book is a primer on how to end your headaches about getting into college and how to afford it without taking the off-ramp to retirement delay.

In the admissions process, this book assumes your child is competing against other students with the same grades and test scores, and with every intention of applying to the same colleges and universities. It doesn't matter what quality of school you're considering. Your student is already at a disadvantage because the competition is *sameness*. It's because of sameness that the Ivy League schools reject over 85% of their applicants who have the *same* terrific grades and test scores. It's a damaging sameness because it damages a student's chances of standing out from all other applicants who look the same. That makes it more difficult for the admissions office to admit your student.

What can this book do for you? It can't change your child's grades or test scores, which can easily represent 85% of the admission decision; however, what it will guarantee is that your son or daughter will receive special attention in the admissions office, thereby eliminating the stigma of *sameness*. I'll show you proven ways to market your child so it's easier to get into the right-fit college of his or her choice. All you have to do is follow my suggestions.

Getting into college and affording it begins with good marketing, or "packaging." On the surface, packaging looks distasteful and dishonest, and that merit should be the only reason why a student gets accepted. But how a student presents himself and his credentials can mean the difference between acceptance and rejection. Colleges already see your student as a product they want to buy. You can use this book to help "sell" your child to colleges. On the other hand, I suggest no attempt at programming your student. Instead, I offer guidelines and suggestions on what to say and do that have proven to work. What's most important is that your student be honest and personal, as well as thoughtful and focused. Plus, retirement will never again look so far away.

At this moment, you may feel like a bewildered boat passenger on rough seas, but this book will guide you in the right direction and into smooth waters. The most important advice I can give you is to allow your child to demonstrate maturity: when there are questions that need answers, have your student do the asking and get the answers. You can be a passenger on this ship, but let your student be the captain with this book as his or her compass. It'll be a beneficial life experience as he or she navigates carefully around the larger islands of Responsibility and Maturity, as well as the smaller islands of Detail, Creativity, Initiative, and Courtesy.

In the financial aid process, you will discover the boneheaded thinking of college administrators. In spite of them, the money-saving ideas and strategies here have already been tested and proven. These ideas have saved parents thousands of dollars per child in college costs. One section of this book will demonstrate how any parent - brace yourself - can pay absolutely nothing for their child's college education, and that's without ever receiving a single scholarship from any source. There's some uncommon common sense in these pages.

On the flip side, the most harebrained suggestion I could offer is for you to do this alone. Your buying this book is like getting a driving manual for your new and expensive car. Along with this book, here's your bonus: *you get me*. Call me anytime for help in protecting your chariot of the gods.

My objective for you and your student is not simply to win, but to use the same plotting commitment that characterizes the colleges themselves: to win, and win big.

Planning For College

Economics 101
College Is Resume-Building Time

1. Supply and Demand. Use these next 2 pages as talking points for a serious sit-down discussion with your student about economics. Begin by stating that you may not have the money (supply) to send him/her to the college s/he wants to attend (demand). This brings you both to...

2. Basic Economic Principles: Regardless of income, one principle is a constant: your income has limits, which means you're limited to what you can spend. Before your children go off to college each fall, make certain they have a summer job that earns them spending money for the following year. By not sending them a dime during the school year will force them to learn how to budget their money, a valuable economics lesson they won't learn from a professor (Can you believe it?). This is your helpful way of immersing them in the real world that starts immediately, not after graduation. It's also a real-life, genuine selling feature that your student can put on a resume. It's a powerful statement before each job interview, "I have 4 years of experience in money-management." What's that worth to an employer?

3. Capital and Labor: Discuss the choice of a college major, and the impact a poorly chosen career can have on income, life-style - the pursuit of happiness. Discuss how an enjoyable and satisfying career can produce the money needed to purchase real freedom. This may be your biggest challenge: we live in a high-tech nation of plugged-in and cyber-connected kids who find it hard to grasp that a self-fulfilling life is not about the pursuit of things that rust. If you can define Jefferson's pursuit of happiness, that your child's life deserves meaning and value, s/he'll be more focused on things that really matter. What's that worth to your student?

4. Competition and Production: Students grasp what it means to compete and produce. After you pick your college, fix your aim on graduating with honors. Why raise the bar of expectations? Because that's what the real world of competition does. It's also your chance to get the extra recognition for the extra effort, to earn yourself a higher degree of self-confidence, and a greater sense of pride. It's another powerful statement your child needs to communicate before all job interviews: "I know how to focus, how to compete, how to succeed, and I have a productive work ethic." What's all this worth to an employer? To you?

5. Forces and Indicators: Simple honesty about you can make a positive impression on an admissions director (not to mention all other earthlings). "In 20 years," says a mid-West director of admissions, "the most refreshing attribute I've seen is [applicants'] recognition of their successes and failures....I'm looking for [your] ability to recognize your shortcomings and fix them." For example, discuss a bad grade and tell the director specifically what you did, or will do, to fix it. Or, admit right up front that your SATs are poor, but you work hard and you're a good student.

To go back to the same admission officer with evidence of actual progress, begin visiting colleges not later than April of your junior year. Your goal is to stand out from all the rest, be noticed and be admitted.

6. The Bottom Line: College is the real world. Like medical interns who train and practice their craft in real-world hospitals, college is a real practice-run for life after graduation. If they have practiced well, your children will do well, no matter what college they attend. See section, *Ask Tough Questions*, item #2.

"In 18 years of in-the-trenches experience counseling kids on their college choices, I've never seen the unhappiness as widespread as it is today. If colleges don't tone down the politics, and figure out how to control ballooning costs, they run the risk of turning off enough American consumers that many campuses could marginalize themselves right out of existence."

Steven Roy Goodman
"Hey, Profs, Come Back to Earth"
Washington Post, 4 /10 /2005

"Approximately one-third of all colleges and universities have financial statements that are significantly weaker than they were several years ago....The translation: Institutions have more liabilities, higher debt service and increasing expense without the revenue or the cash reserves to back them up."

The Financially Sustainable University
Bain & Company, 2012

Is Your Child A WMD?
Be Careful What You Promise

A client told me that he raised a very independent-minded son. He was offered $8,500 from one college, which the son liked, and $21,000 from a school the father liked. Guess which school was chosen by independent-minded? The father told me the son's choice was going to cost him an additional $12,500 a year, or an additional $50,000 over 4 years. With money intended for the winter of his years, daddy unknowingly raised a little weapon of mass destruction of his retirement.

Because it was a family tradition, the father always promised independent-minded that he could go to the college of his choice. Tradition was getting a hernia, and his promise became an exit ramp to retirement delay. Last we heard, the son's having a great time at school, and his grades are somewhere south of Acceptable.

TIP #1: Before your child gives you spasms of retirement heartburn, set specific parameters, such as making sure an offer for $21,000 won't be overridden by a smaller award that comes with more beer and cheer. With too much money at stake, common sense must rule the day. There are over 4,000 colleges in America, and there are a lot more colleges that'll give you and your child what you both want.

TIP #2: I hesitated with this one. This worked for a client, so she claims, who suggested that raindrops can solve a big college-selection headache. If your child wants to go to a college that has you reaching for the antacids, and your student wants to see the campus, select a rainy day to visit, and forget to bring the umbrella. Getting wet in lousy weather will insinuate a negative impression of the school. Like I said, I hesitated with this one.

2 Dirty Secrets

Don't Trust The People Who Send The Bill

Never assume that a college president is a master craftsman of a logical thought. One president, whose university has an endowment (cash stash) of $313,000,000, declared his school's way of increasing financial aid is to increase tuition. In other words, he's increasing your financial aid package by $500, but to do so he's increasing your tuition by $1,500. Get it? I don't either.

Note the wording in the title of this newspaper headline: "Univ of Washington Considers High Tuition - High Aid Model." There's actually a formula - a model - colleges use to raise tuitions! And college presidents, once society's beacons of social conscience and enlightenment, are nothing more than no-profile and over-paid fund-raisers.

Dirty Secret #1: Students who don't need as much financial aid as you do will get some of your tuition increase. Why? Either to attract smarter students or high-income students. What's wrong with this picture? Aren't smarter, low-income students supposed to get more aid? The trend, according to the National Postsecondary Student Aid Survey, indicates that many colleges are taking the ruthless approach that says, "Poor students bring in far less revenue than rich ones. To get the rich kids to pay us more money, let's entice them with a little financial aid so they can pay a little less to attend, but pay a whole lot more than poor students."

Higher income families receive more financial aid at a rate four times more than students who traditionally would qualify for more aid under most need-based formulas. At the College of Greed, some traditions die with the greatest of ease.

Even though 51% of high-income families are receiving more grant aid - free money, is it possible that the standards for merit aid - higher grades and higher test scores - have loosened? Colleges will publish their high standards, but it doesn't mean they adhere to them. Perish the thought. It can easily be argued that the standards are adjusted, with moral relativism as Gatorade for the college game, in order for the money to flow more easily to school treasuries, or become one of the growing number of billion-dollar endowment universities.

Dirty Secret #2: It's the reverse of Dirty Secret #1. You could be subsidizing someone else's kid who's considered smarter than yours, but who needs *more* financial aid. The budget director at a university in Washington suggested to other colleges, "...boost tuition, but follow it with a hike in financial aid for needy students." So your child, who is more talented than most, gets more financial aid (read: larger discount) because you're from a low-income family on whose behalf some colleges will rob from high-income families.

Deception and cynicism permeate the rules of the college game. Colleges claim to recruit students from low-income families, but they've concluded that very few talented students come from poverty environments. A former Ivy League school admissions officer labels such a student as a "quintessential diamond in the rough." Translation: it's rare to find someone intelligent in ghettos. It seems the strategy is not to recruit more low-income students, but to give the politically correct and bogus impression that no child is left behind. It's far cheaper to issue self-serving press releases than to award merit scholarships.

What really works for colleges is economic discrimination, no matter how ruthless it functions, or how ugly it looks. It's okay to play dirty. And appearances nearly always trump values.

When there was a congressional proposal to make colleges prove they're well-run and deliver value, that was a bad idea according to a college president and head of the Association of American Colleges and Universities. It's a proposal, he says, "that no reasonable person would want to support." So parents who work 2 to 3 jobs, risking their retirements everyday to pay for skyrocketing tuition increases every year, are unreasonable. Too many college presidents are simply clueless.

"I feel deeply sympathetic," a college president declares, "with the challenge these kinds of increases pose to parents, and we do our best to keep expenses down as much as we can." Deeply sympathetic? Keep expenses down? As Fox TV's John Stossel would say, "Give me a break!" What's alarming is that this official actually believes what he says. Or does he? If he doesn't, parents are in more trouble than I thought.

A university whose endowment exceeded 1 BILLION dollars in 2007 wrote the following statement to a student from its Office of Financial Assistance: "*Since our sources are limited* (Italics added), funds must be given to students with greater demonstrated need." After reading this twaddle, I had a John Stossel moment.

A Catholic college in Boston was shameless in a logic that was baffling and backwards. Three news stories appeared in the following sequence: the first announced its new status as a *billion*-dollar endowment university; the second said the school purchased more real estate for 214 million dollars because of its ability to pay cash up front; and the third story - brace yourself - stated that since "excellence is an expensive proposition," along with rising energy and insurance costs, tuition and fees must increase to $44,226 a year (2006). Arrogance is a blinding mechanism that crafts the illogical to appear logical. In 2014, this college's cost of attendance went to $60,720.

Imagine Donald Trump demanding more money for "excellence" and expenses, when earlier he boasted of his one billion dollars in profitable investments that allowed him to pay cash up front for his latest and very expensive purchase. Colleges well deserve our skepticism (I wanted to use the word "contempt," but my brothers-in-law are graduates of the school; I like their invites during holidays).

Given the mindset of those in charge of the college game, anchored squarely in a moral sinkhole, I'm asking only one question: Are the colleges trying to fool some of the parents and students some of the time, some of the parents and students all of the time, or all of the parents and students all of the time?

You pay, you decide.

_____

"Universities share one characteristic with compulsive gamblers and exiled royalty: there is never enough money to satisfy their desires."

Derek Bok, former president, Harvard University

Ask Tough Questions
Get In Their Faces

Before reading the following, you may want to take two minutes to breathe into a brown paper bag.

A so-called "prestigious" university in Washington DC guaranteed the class of 2020 the same tuition price for up to 5 years, but the price for the cost of attendance each year (including books, personal and living expenses) will be $66,310 per year. And they'll get it all with a short, written notice instead of a short, muzzled revolver. The time has finally arrived to view the IRS as the Good Guys.

The incredibly out-of-touch financial aid director of this university announced: "Generally, families feel more comfortable knowing the financial obligations to the university in advance of matriculating." I get it. I should feel more comfortable knowing the caliber of the gun pointed at my head in advance of your pulling the trigger.

Colleges have no incentive to lower costs since more and more students continue to apply. For the class of 2019, New York University received over 50,000 applications for less than 6,000 openings. Increasingly, colleges exercise their own Golden Rule: as your child goes for the gold, we rule.

Ask these 3 tough questions (among many) before applying to any college:

(1) Will my child be taught by full-time professors? To cut their costs, not yours, more and more colleges are hiring part-time faculty for less pay to do most of the teaching. Over half of all college faculties are part-timers, up from only 22% in 1970. Plus, "universities neglect undergraduate teaching," concludes an observer of American higher education, Dr. Ron Melcher of the University of Ottawa, and "excessively large classes taught by the least qualified, inexperienced, non-tenured and poorly supported faculty and delivered in impersonal ways are the new norm." Graduate students, also hired as teaching assistants, may speak English as a second language. In short, universities are outsourcing what you thought was promised in their slick catalogs.

The college catalog is a Reader's Digest warrantee that would make fiction writers blush. If a university doesn't have a set policy requiring full-time faculty members to teach your student, a small college could well be a better choice.

Here's a typical college's position toward applying students: *because of our huge pool of applicants, we don't need you.* Your attitude must be a perfect match: because of the huge pool of colleges, I don't need your college. Winning the college game requires that you wear emotional body armor.

(2) Do I want the best college for my child? A Princeton study concluded that bright kids do well no matter where they go to school. Regardless of the school you attend, intelligence, like cream, rises to the top. Approximately 10% of America's largest companies are run by Ivy League grads. Graduating from college, not where you attended, is an economic priority. With today's workplace realities, prospective students for the Ivy League are now saying, "Forget it!"

Can it be ignored that a respect for learning and character has something to do with success and the pursuit of happiness?

Because your student lives in a culture of brand names, they could obsess with going to a name-brand college. To avoid self-inflicted poverty by sending them to a college you cannot afford, indulge the obsession by purchasing the college's sweatshirt. Okay, so my suggestion is dumb, but maybe Miss Brand Name will get the point that your retirement takes priority. Revisit this book's first section, *Economics 101*.

(3) Will I have to sell my yacht, fire two of my servants, or make another million? If your child is an academic superstar, *regardless of your income,* colleges with merit-based aid could give you a minimum of $20,000 in free money (read: discount). Before applying, if you think your student has a chance, ask the college if they have merit-based aid that doesn't require a tie-in to need-based aid, and then get a satisfactory answer to Question #1. To win this college game can certainly be on your terms. Don't sell the yacht.

The 4-Letter Word
Is A Financial Aid Office Really Helpful?

People who work in college financial aid offices are dedicated loan activists who preach the Gospel of Loan, the sacred 4-letter word they always use before they give you any of their money (read: discount). Many of these people are students on a work-study program, which should tell you already that you're talking to the wrong people. Ask for either the director of financial aid or for a financial aid officer (FAO), but beware. Typically oblivious to the economic demands on parents, an FAO at a so-called prestigious college in Maine was asked about the college's reaching the $40,000-a-year mark in 2005. His response was totally clueless: "I think there will become a point where cost is a major factor, but I don't know if $40,000 is that point." He doesn't know? Either his brain has atrophied from sniffing too much cash, he's lost in the vast Maine woods, or he's not a parent. This school's cost of attendance in 2016 is $63,880, which equals the predictable yearly increase of 5-to-6 percent. I'll bet this dude doesn't know if $70,000 "is that point."

FAOs are woefully ignorant of how to finance an education without regurgitating the 4-letter word. These are the same people who conduct financial aid nights at your local high school. Talk about the blind leading the blind. It gets worse.

The Boston Globe said that colleges are trying to "shed the image of financial aid offices and their advisers as cold and intimidating. Two years ago, [a college in Boston] renovated its financial service center to give it warmth, hoping to soothe the nerves of students and parents wrestling with how to pay for school." Translation: "We wouldn't rob you with a gun, we do it with a potted plant instead."

They're warm and fuzzy when you lose your job and can't pay next semester's bill. Colleges may help you with additional aid (read: loan) so your child isn't forced to leave. It's nothing more than a business strategy to protect the college's keep-'em-at-any-cost retention rate. It has little or nothing to do with compassion. See section, **Getting The Most Aid.**

When you read those great advice columns on financial aid, you'll be told that the first thing you should do is contact the financial aid office. It's great advice if you want to abuse yourself by getting into more debt with another loan.

The Cost Of Diversity
Self-Righteous Fraud

When you read the word "diversity" in a college's literature, hold your nose. The foul odor originates from what you don't see. And my political incorrectness may be hard to swallow. I'm crossing my fingers...

Illegal Aliens Your tax and tuition dollars may pay for an illegal alien to attend class with your child. To follow 16 other states which defy federal law, your state's politicians may allow illegal aliens to pay the same in-state tuition costs at state schools as American-born state residents. Message to illegals: break our laws and we'll reward you with in-state tuition prices. With trademark credentials for pandering, many politicians act as if illegal aliens add to the rich diversity of our colleges and universities.

Same-Sex Couples They pay less than typical parents. According to the tax laws, same-sex couples are single parents, and a single parent can qualify for more aid. The politically-correct National Association of Student Financial Aid Administrators is *suggesting* - brace yourself - that colleges "invite same-sex couples to be honest" in filling out aid forms. When same-sex couples can simply obey the law by using one tax return to verify household income, what's their incentive to be honest in disclosing two incomes? I'm guessing the invitation to be honest will be accepted when all hell freezes over.

Affirmative Action From the LA Times: "Affirmative action is highly unpopular...92% of the public (86% of blacks) agreed that admissions, hiring and promotion decisions 'should be based strictly on merit and qualifications other than race/ethnicity.' *Only bureaucrats and intellectuals...love affirmative action*" (Italics added). Your child can be the ideal candidate for a college that prides itself on its "diversity," but if the college has already met its quota of white, Asian, Jewish, Hispanic, in-state, out-of-state, or legacy students, you could be a loser. Whoever thought that a hard-working student who deserves admission for outstanding achievement could be passed over by someone else's skin color, ethnic group, or geography? A 2004 Princeton study concluded that "elite" colleges give black applicants "the equivalent of 230 extra SAT points," and Hispanics get another 185 points.

Colleges like to be miniature versions of the United Nations. Appearances transcend substance. A college campus *appears* to be a magnet that draws students from all over the world. What you see is not by accident, it's by design. Racial and ethnic discrimination are firmly in place in order for diversity to exist. There's little evidence that college administrators are racists, but the end results have all the ugly signs of what both cynics and the can't-we-all-get-along crowd call "good racism." In the admissions office, good racism is allowed to get in the way of proven, hard-working talent.

Apply to your match and safety schools (certainly not reach schools) on an Early Action basis, not Early Decision (See section, *EarlyEarlyEarlyEarlyEarly*). And do it after Labor Day before the herd applies in December. Be the first male, female, athlete, Asian, Jew, rich, poor, out-of-state, in-state, violinist, white, black, American Indian, drawf, albino, legacy, piano player, or child-of-donor student to apply. Your chances of getting admitted are better if you're the first to begin filling a quota that matches a predetermined profile. If the quota has already been met, you're toast. Timing is everything.

Gender Balance With men more likely to drop out, women are assets and men are liabilities. For every 100 graduates, 58 are daughters and 42 are sons. Where T-shirts can be found to say, "Girls rule, boys drool," you'd think colleges aim for more gender balance. They don't. Kenyon College admissions dean, Jennifer D. Britz, claims that "young men are rarer, they're more valued applicants." But her college isn't running enrollment ads for more male students. Lip service trumps male recruitment efforts across the land. Colleges don't dare admit to practicing sex discrimination. According to Alex Kingsbury of US News & World Report, this is the collegiate perspective on women: "Girls watch less television, spend less time playing sports, and are far less likely to find themselves in detention. They are more likely to participate in drama, art, and music classes — extracurriculars that are catnip for admissions officers. Across the board, girls study more, score better, and are less likely to be placed in special education classes." In other words, babes rock and jocks slobber. But in a college's quest for "balance," hormonally imbalanced 18-year-old guys - aren't they all? - will trip all over themselves to apply where the babes are, thereby tipping the balance toward parity. Cue the music of the 1960s rock 'n roll group, the Beach Boys: "Two girls for ev-vry boy...."

Poor Students "Increasingly, discounts [scholarships] go not mainly to low-income students," claims economist Richard Vedder of Ohio State, "but to talented students prized by universities seeking to improve ratings on the athletic field or in the U.S. News & World

Report rankings." Colleges prefer the rich who can pay the bills, but if they're going to give aid to a poor student, preference will go to an academic superstar. With over 80 colleges boasting of their billion-dollar endowments, only 6 have *plans* to help poor families. Or, 90% have no plans at all. See section, *2 Dirty Secrets.*

Intellectual Discrimination So far the definition of college diversity includes acceptable criminal behavior, racial discrimination, economic discrimination, and sex discrimination. Who said college isn't the real world? To make matters worse, there's intellectual discrimination. Nearly 75% of all college professors hold the same political ideology, and evidence mounts that students who raise opposing views in the classroom risk getting lower grades. "Inbred ideological narrowness shows up," says columnist Thomas Sowell, "not only in hiring and teaching, but also in restrictive campus speech codes for students, created by the very academics who complain loudly when their own 'free speech' is challenged."

For parents and students, college diversity is an expensive fraud. A radical polarization of thinking should occur only after you've been mugged on a dark street, not in a college classroom. Like it or not, to maintain a college's cosmetic diversity and its religious zeal for political correctness, instead of a constant nurturing and open exchange of ideas, it has become a student's and parent's take-it-or-leave-it obligation to pay through the nose. And, as Ohio State's professor Vedder said of college teaching in a TV interview: "With the possible exception of prostitution, there is no other profession that has had absolutely no productivity advance since Socrates taught the youth of Athens."

To reduce your costs without using your nose as a conduit, continue reading.

Admissions 101
What Colleges Want: The Top 10

"1. A high school curriculum that challenges the student... students should include...Honors and Advanced Placement classes.

"2. ...Grades should show an upward trend over the years. However, slightly lower grades in a rigorous program are preferred to all A's in less challenging coursework.

"3. Solid scores on standardized tests (SAT, ACT). These should be consistent with high school performance.

"4. Passionate involvement in a few activities, demonstrating leadership and initiative. Depth, not breadth...is most important.

"5. Community service showing evidence of being a 'contributor.' Activities should demonstrate concern for other people.

"6. Out-of-school experiences (including summer activities) that illustrate responsibility, dedication and development of areas of interest. Work or meaningful use of free time demonstrates maturity.

"7. A well-written essay that provides insight into the student's unique personality, values and goals. The application essay should be thoughtful and highly personal.

"8. Letters of recommendation from teachers and guidance counselor that give evidence of integrity, special skill, and positive character traits. Students should request recommendations from teachers who respect their work in an academic discipline.

"9. Supplementary recommendations by adults who have had significant direct contact with the student. Letters from coaches or supervisors in long-term work or volunteer activities are valuable; however, recommendations from casual acquaintances or family friends, even if they are well known, are rarely given much weight.

"10. Anything special that makes the student stand out from the rest of the applicants! Include honors, awards, evidence of unusual talent or experience.... Overall, colleges are seeking students who will be active contributing members of the student body."

Source: survey from a national independent group of college admissions pros.

Before The Junior Year

Do Something.

Begin the admissions process no later than the 9th grade. When your child's applications arrive in the room of the admissions committee 4 years later, it's Showtime: the decision to admit your student will take no longer than 30 minutes. "Today, it's a complicated and prolonged dance that begins early," says J. D. Britz, dean of admissions and financial aid of Kenyon College..."there is little margin for error: A grade of C in Algebra II/Trig? Off to the wait-list you go."

Olympic athletes begin practicing their sport 4 years before their Showtime, which takes a lot less than 30 minutes with little margin for error. Your student's preparation for admission success will take the form of fatigue, long hours, boredom, and little recognition until their Showtime. The difference is that your student will more likely win the gold, which means admission.

As an Olympic athlete must practice for only one event with total commitment, *a student should specialize in one activity or talent that demonstrates a real interest, passion, or the student's uniqueness.* Limiting focus will allow for more time to study and to improve grades. Creating a limited but strong profile - a theme - gives the colleges what they desire.

The student's mission is two-fold: to get good grades and to demonstrate commitment to what interests you most. While schools use grades and test scores to *qualify* you for admission, what must you do to be *accepted*? Engage in very few but quality activities that demonstrate your theme, such as community service projects which you originate, organize and continue to nurture. Or commit enthusiastically in one sport or one club with the sole objective of being its captain or being an officer.

A college admissions committee wants to see how you've managed your time and focused your efforts. Colleges want to see evidence of your passion for *something.* Having a single purpose is in, being well-rounded is out.

For non-academic activities, there's a terrific website that's a cyberspace substitute for an inspiring parent. Teens relate to it and use it. It makes "community service as cool as sports." This is great news for the shy and timid student.

This website promotes young people engaging in "creating organizations, programs, and initiatives, and/or building upon existing programs." It's not so important that you join something as much as you create something that gets others to join your something. The website speaks for itself:

> "You have a lot of ideas about how you'd like to change the world or at least you have a lot of questions and concerns and you're looking for specific things you can do. We're giving you a place to connect, a place to be inspired, be supported, be celebrated. The only question is, 'What's your something?'"

"**Do Something** has contracted with DeHavilland Associates to conduct an independent evaluation of program impact. Educators assess their students' growth on leadership, citizenship, and character skills alongside academic skill development through assessment tools provided by **Do Something**. These results are collected and analyzed by DeHavilland to document our impact.

"Educators have also told us that participating in **Do Something** leads to powerful outcomes for young people:

91% say **Do Something** increases self-confidence

61% say **Do Something** increases students' academic performance and reduces school discipline problems

87% say **Do Something** increases student and staff morale, and

77% say **Do Something** increases parental and community involvement at school."

If you don't know what to do in high school to get another all-important edge for college admission, put down this book right now and go to this website: www.dosomething.org. Oh! There's one other recommendation: revisit this site often.

If Your Child Is A High School Junior...
Don't Wait Anymore

1. Use These 3 Websites Before You Do Anything.
Both students and parents should go online to Triangle Education Assessments and get their MBTI-Strong career package. It is the near-scientific way to "find yourself." The extraordinary people who run this website help discover your behavioral DNA: your motivations, style, needs, and stress points in order to find the best-fit careers. It is so foundational that it renders obsolete all popular and free methods of determining a college major. Once you acknowledge who you are, you can effectively choose which career match is the best fit for you. At this point, go to collegeboard.com for the major which matches those careers. Once there, click in this sequence: For Students > Find A College > Majors and Careers. When finished, go to www.princetonreview.com and its Counselor-O-Matic. Answer a few questions (use a score of 550 if you haven't taken the SAT I) to match yourself with "reach," "match," and "safety" schools. Choosing a career, a college major, and the right-fit school just got a whole lot easier and a whole lot less expensive. Picking a school based on spectacular mailbox literature, impressive websites, or Thirsty Thursdays is risky. Your child doesn't have to be part of the 31% of entering freshmen who drop out after the first year, or part of near 70% who need more than 4 years to graduate.

After deciding your college choices, visit campuses to get a solid feeling for each school, but first start by visiting this website: CampusTours.com.

These questions can be answered before you apply by visiting the schools which match your career inclinations. A curriculum-match has far greater importance than a brand-name school. See section, *Ask Tough Questions*.

An overnight college visit (during the school week) always weighs in the student's favor. Plan your visit to include an appointment with the department head of your preferred major (with questions not answered on the college's website), and/or plan on attending 2 classes the next morning before you head over to the admissions office to say "Thanks." Set an appointment for a follow-up interview, *if required*. If you traveled a very long distance, the interview should be scheduled along with your visit. If you live not more than a 3-hour trip away, a second visit communicates a very strong interest, and

40

that'll impress the admissions person who may decide your fate. **Caution**: Don't post your student's fun photos on these websites: Facebook and Instagram. Pics with lots of flesh and parties could cause a resentful but anonymous classmate to notify a school of your student's unseemly behavior.

The interview is good face-time with the admissions person in charge of your application, who can put a face to your application when decision-time comes. Parents should be on the side-lines during the visit, leaving the student alone and totally undistracted.

If you have a great essay (See section, *How To Apply To College*), you'll move very fast to being accepted. Start planning your visitation dates with colleges, and apply Early Action to matching and safety schools so your last visit is no later than the first week of December of your senior year.

2. Get Better Test Scores. Hire A Private Tutor.
When a college receives applications from two students with near similar grades and comparable extra-curricular activities, guess who gets picked? It's the ultimate tie-breaker with schools that don't require SAT or ACT scores. See section, *SAT & ACT.*

3. Take Honors & AP Classes.
You can qualify for college credit by taking these courses. If you score 4 or better on the AP (Advanced Placement) exam, you can receive college credit and save as much as $4,500 per course at a private college. Getting B's in Honors or AP classes, instead of A's in regular courses, will look better on a transcript. The colleges will see that you challenged yourself by taking something harder to get to college rather than taking something easier to get to graduation. Proof of challenging yourself beats an easy A every time.

If you didn't take an AP course, get a support letter of your ability to handle such a course from your guidance office and take a course at a nearby college during the summer between your junior and senior years. You get 4 positive benefits: (1) prospective colleges will be very impressed that you had the initiative and maturity to challenge yourself to get (2) college credit; (3) you get first-hand knowledge of a college classroom experience, something that few or none of your classmates will claim; and (4) your letters of recommendation will reinforce #1.

4. Reposition Assets & Personal Finances Now.

Do you know how to lower the value of your home in the eyes of private schools in order to qualify for more aid? Do you have money saved in your child's name? Do you have money saved in a mattress? Will you put money into a universal life insurance policy?

A simple mistake in how you handle any of the above situations could be very expensive. Take control of the process, but it's a Herculean task that's better left to a professional in the field of financial aid. Only then can you use legal and ethical strategies to reduce the amount of money the schools will expect you to pay.

The last date you should reposition assets to avoid financial aid penalties is December 31st of the **junior** year when you're applying to schools that only require the FAFSA (most state colleges). The timing of repositioning avoids any look-back by a college searching for assets. Move them completely by December 31st of the **sophomore** year if you're applying to colleges which also require the CSS Profile. You may not have to abide by this guideline since many financial aid officers don't give the hardest scrutiny to financial statements; however, your top schools train a pedigree of eagles with eyes to spot the smallest questionable entry. See section, *Asset Strategies*.

Notify your accountant that you want to be at the top of his list of tax returns to be completed after the first of the year. Let him know that financial aid is a very time-sensitive issue because financial aid from the schools (separate from Uncle Sam) is awarded on a first-come, first-served basis. The same request goes to anyone else who has control over your tax return. Timing is everything.

To get a detailed by-the-month list (make a print-out) of what needs to be done during the junior year, go to this website: www.nacac-net.org. Once you're there, click on these items in the following sequence: Student Resources > College Preparation > Junior Year Calendar.

If Your Child Is A High School Senior...

Some Financial Questions Must Be Asked Now

If your child hasn't started filling out college applications, do it now. For admissions issues, see section, *How To Apply To College.* For now, ask a college financial aid office some simple questions:

What % of my need does your school meet?
Only the most selective colleges are likely to meet 100% of a student's financial need. Know this information in advance before your child spends time applying to a particular school that will *never* give you the money you need.

For the amount of need met by nearly all colleges, go to www.collegeboard.com. Click in the following sequence: For Parents > College Search > College QuickFinder (and then the first letter of school's name) > Cost & Financial Aid. Caution: this information indicates an average; if your student doesn't match the average but is accepted anyway, you won't be offered the average.

Do I get the same aid package all 4 years?
A school may offer a student a great package in the first year. In the following year, it may offer the same package, but in different ratios, that is, more loans and less grants. It's likely since such an offer smells of a bait-and-switch move. That's because it is. To be on the safe side, ask the school what their policy is for the second, third and fourth years. Nail down the ratios. If the school gives you the answer you want to hear, you'll see it in the award letter. Award letters typically indicate that the school's award offer is good all four years, providing you maintain a certain grade-point average and you remain in school for four consecutive years.

Will my aid be adjusted if my need changes?
Some schools will not adjust a student's financial aid package after the first year, regardless of what happens to your finances in succeeding years. This becomes a serious problem especially if the family's income drops in the later years of college. Know the school's policy in advance so your student won't have to drop out later.

If I don't apply for financial aid before the freshman year, can I apply later?

You can always apply later. In some cases it may make sense for you not to apply for aid for the freshman year, especially if you haven't done any planning, and all of your assets are in the wrong places.

If you're a transfer student, some schools have policies of giving priority consideration to students who are already attending and receiving financial aid. If this is the school's policy, you may be shut out from getting help. Forget policy. Go ahead and appeal your award anyway. You won't know the results unless you ask.

Never volunteer any financial information on the phone to a college financial aid officer. Let your required forms do the talking. On how to answer their phone call, see section, *After The Award Letters*.

After entering college, you'll have to fill out the FAFSA form each year. Your punishment is mandatory.

Any cut-off dates for guaranteeing financial aid?
I always recommend meeting the school's cut-off date even though the date is a soft deadline. If 1,000 applications show up on the cut-off date, do you suppose each of those applications will be reviewed that day? Hardly. But aim for the cut-off date; lots of schools look for your postmark date. If you're going to be late, it looks a whole lot better if you submit a legitimate reason. The dog-ate-my-application excuse will be well received as the Laugh of the Day, but I wouldn't suggest it.

To get a detailed by-the-month list (make a print-out) of what needs to be done during the senior year, go to this website: www.nacac-net.org. Once you're there, click on these items in the following sequence: Student Resources > College Preparation > Senior Year Calendar.

See section, *What You Absolutely Must Do Right Now...* near the back of this book.

"...one can't help but wonder if the cost of a college education at many institutions isn't vastly out of line with the educational value delivered."   *Jay Matthews, Washington Post*

How & Where To Get Free Money
As Colleges Sell Sizzle, Look For Steak

With yearly tuition increases exceeding twice the rate of inflation, aid packages contain a lot more loans than grants. Before applying to Our Lady of Perpetual Increase University, consider these 5 recommendations:

1. Look for the steak, ignore the sizzle. Financial aid is nothing more than a game played by someone else's rules and on their playing field. Your opponent believes you're clueless. Protect yourself with a skeptical attitude, which comes with being better informed. Just by looking at their stunning websites, you can conclude colleges are experts at selling sizzle in the thoughtless expectation you won't wince at the price. Your best defense is to focus on the steak. How?

2. Ignore the frills. Colleges want to appeal, not to young, developing minds, but to their crass instincts. Here's the college marketing mentality: let's go for the lower common denominators to attract students. Instead of bragging of its two Shakespeare scholars, a university in New England boasts of its multi-million dollar swimming pool with a wave machine. An engineering school in New York prefers to advertise the presence of a Starbucks on campus, instead of its Nobel Laureate. The nation's #1 party school has a massage parlor so students can relieve stress (I'm not making this up!); and, of course, every school must have a state-of-the-art gym. One Ohio university spent $140 million dollars on a sports complex that features canoes, batting cages, massages, and a climbing wall big enough to handle 50 students. Prediction: within 20 years, Disney World will be out of business because the colleges and universities will be local entertainment magnets that will match Disney's amusement amenities.

3. Go shopping... Don't waste your time traveling to a beautiful campus whose aid plan is weighted heavily towards loans. Ball State University's published aid-package ratio approximates 60% loans to 40% grants, whereas Stonehill College's is 60% grants to 40% loans. Two good schools, but one better aid package (steak). Making choices just got a whole lot easier. But where's the beef?

4. ...at this info market. Here's a huge steak tip: to discover who has better grant-to-loan ratios, go to www.collegeboard.com and do a college search. Go to the school's *Cost & Financial Aid* and look for the *average percent of need met*.

Colleges which don't disclose this statistical information are the first to tell you that they treat everyone as an individual, not as a statistic. It's the first sign that you're about to be snookered. If a college can't make the slightest effort to help you make an informed decision on something as simple as their grant-to-loan ratio, perhaps the school should be off your radar screen of choices. Then again, many of these offices are filled with uninformed students on work-study.

5. Hire a private tutor. Higher SAT/ACT scores can mean more grant money from private colleges. Many will give you grants starting at $20,000 if SATs are just over 1100 (excluding the Writing section) and you're in the top 20% of your class. Children of millionaires can get this money. Visit the college's website, click on "Financial Aid," and look for the school's scholarships that list their requirements. See section, *SAT & ACT.*

Colleges want you to believe - ready for this? - there's more to choosing a college than just money. Don't be fooled. Colleges are in the game of marketing their own banquet of sizzle, and if Stonehill can do the same for your child as Ball State, your choice is easy. There are plenty of good schools like Ball State, but with better aid packages like Stonehill's. With growing endowments, private colleges are private banks. That's where the money is. More steak, please.

Grant and scholarship monies are awarded mostly on merit (great grades and test scores) rather than need. This money is donated by corporations, alumni, government, or the college. It's simply a discount off the sticker price.

If you don't receive a discount, it may be due to (a) your child's in the bottom 50% of the entering class, (b) you don't qualify for need-based aid, (c) you qualify for lots of financial aid, but were late in submitting your aid forms, (d) you were on-time but the forms had the usual errors, omissions, and inconsistencies, or (e) you were one of the 1.8 million families who didn't fill out any forms. The life-isn't-fair response won't work. What works is doing everything right the first time. To get started, revisit item #4.

Bad Advice
Unrealistic, Half True, Or Flat-Out Wrong

Beware of the so-called experts.

Advice in newspapers. From the Washington Post: "The first place experts recommend that students and their families turn is the financial aid office at their college." Not even the Washington Post knows, nor should it be expected to know, that the last people you should talk to are in the financial aid office. Why? Because these people are hard-core loan activists who work in the very expensive business of academic services and away-from-home frills. Why would you call a financial aid office when more debt will be suggested? Would you call the IRS for advice on how to reduce your taxes?

Here's bad advice from a Wall Street Journal article: "...it is wise to minimize the amount of funds that appear available in the eyes of financial-aid administrators by *paying off* large consumer debts, such as credit-card and car-loan balances." It's wise to minimize, but you don't have to spend. You could do gifting instead. See section, *Asset Strategies.* Take your daddy's advice: be careful what you read in the newspaper.

Advice in books From the Princeton Review's *Paying For College Without Going Broke,* a young couple with a 3-year-old can put away $4,000 a year for 15 years and "have a college fund in excess of $55,750." But in 15 years, with costs for state colleges increasing by 10% a year, the price tag for the first year at the University of Nebraska will approximate $65,000. The Princeton Review's recommended college fund cannot even pay for the entire first year.

Advice from financial planners (aka stock brokers) From a nationally known author and financial adviser: "Since retirement accounts and your personal residence don't count against you in determining the aid for which your student will qualify, maximize your retirement contributions or make extra payments on your mortgage." This is a classic but dangerous half-truth. It's true that your residence doesn't count against you, but with schools that require only the FAFSA. Typically, these are state schools and lesser-known private colleges. If you're applying to high-profile private schools, most of them will begin to salivate uncontrollably at the discovery that you have home equity. With every $100,000 in equity, you will lose at least $5,000 in aid per year, *per student*, as long as the equity just sits there.

If you're making extra principle payments every month, you're walking towards a meat-grinder with private colleges. If a private school is in your future, stop making those extra payments immediately. See section, *Asset Strategies,* on how to reposition your home equity for more aid.

Flat-Out Wrong In a Boston newspaper article, a financial advisor told readers not to take out a larger mortgage on their home. But he doesn't state why this approach doesn't work. I had a few clients take out a larger mortgage, and in the process of refinancing, they were able to maintain their monthly payments and withdraw enough money to pay for college; this is rare, which is one reason I'm not an advocate if this approach. I repositioned the extra cash in a financial vehicle that's legally invisible to the schools, which is discussed in section, *Asset Strategies*. In many cases, this allows parents to pay less for private colleges than state institutions, which is a golden nugget the financial advisor never dug up for his readers.

There aren't enough college admissions and financial aid experts in the country today. You can't even find one listed in the online yellow pages. I'm not listed because most of my clients are referred to me by other clients, or they found my phone number in this book.

"Hypocrisy, faddishness, arrogance and intellectual cowardice are among the ailments of the American university today... Amid the variety of scandals afflicting the campuses, the one constant is how the rhetoric of 'diversity' trumps almost all other considerations— and how race and gender can be manipulated by either the college president or the faculty in ways that have nothing to do with educating America's youth... There is enormous intellectual arrogance on the campus these days, manifested in condescension towards the average taxpaying citizen."

Victor Davis Hanson
Senior Fellow, Hoover Institution

Your College Application
A Pain In the Class

The *Challenger* space shuttle exploded several years ago because someone didn't pay attention to a known minor detail that causes O-ring seals to expand. Set into motion was an explosion that killed the entire crew. Here's the stark reality for all students: for 3½ years of school work, the admissions committee, like an employer, will give your child's application anywhere from 30 seconds to 30 minutes for a decision. Any errors on the application can set into motion what will kill your student's chances for admission. Since the devil is in the details, you must dance with him with precision and objectivity.

A college application is another test to get into college. It's seductively simple, yet potentially dangerous. When an admissions officer discovers that your student didn't use Spell-check for a couple of misspelled words in the essay, the applicant's future is now at risk. If you're an admissions director overseeing 30,000 applications for 4,000 openings, you can afford to dismiss a bright applicant who's careless.

Message to students: if you don't perform correctly the most simple tasks, your mistakes will distract the admissions officer from making an easy decision in your favor. Message to parents: allow your student to fill out the application, but take extreme care to scrutinize the application before submission. Your student's future could hang by this razor-thin thread.

"Never use the Common Application," insists one admissions and financial aid advisor, "when the college has its own application." In ancient times, as well as today, this is bad advice. More colleges are adopting the Common Application for the ease of completing it. My students definitely prefer it because it allows them to apply to more schools.

The college application may be more important than a job application. Why? Because it decides the dock from which your student will launch his or her life's ship. That dock has to be a solid preparation platform for a future that can be met with confidence. As we say to all of our clients, "Success is in the preparation."

Your student has to look good, and one of the ways to look good is to have an application that looks like a professional document with no mistakes. It sends a potent message to the college that your student went way out of his way to pay strict and careful attention to detail. Result: the applicant stands a far better chance for admission. How hard can this be?

The college application is the first test-run to the first job application after graduation. You must "package" your student to the schools just as the schools package themselves to your student; colleges are selling. The sooner it's done the greater the advantage for acceptance. And your student's thematic paperwork could set the standard by which all other applications, essays, letters of recommendations and resumes are judged. Otherwise, doing what everyone else does will have your student looking like everyone else.

Rejection begins by looking the same as everyone else.

Treat your applying to college as if you're applying for a job. Here's the job title: **College Student**. Your child's resume should begin in the 9th grade. Much to everyone's surprise, the Common Application, which is used by over 500 colleges and universities, has the following requirement: "Briefly list or describe any scholastic distinctions or honors you have won since the ninth grade."

Now that your child is applying for the job position of College Student, the only difference is that paychecks for this job are sent directly to the school. To make a real impact on your young adult, explain the costs involved. For example, if you're spending $25,000 a year for college, divide $25,000 by 140 days of school and the result is $178 a day, 7 days a week, or $1,250 a week. You're paying your child $1,250 a week to live, work, and play (read: drink) away from home. Moreover, remind your student that the weekly salary will increase by 8% each year, which is the tuition increase you'll get from the college. In addition, let your offspring know that when they party every weekend, don't have perfect class attendance, or schedule classes for only 3 days a week, remind them that it's still costing you $1,250 a week, which include days they're not studying.

A student needs a clear perspective on the effort and sacrifice a parent makes on his or her behalf. If your student doesn't produce - maintain good grades - you can give him the Donald Trump blessing...

You're FIRED!

It doesn't matter how much aid you qualify for unless you have a college to attend. To learn more of how to receive help with your student's application, or anything else related to being accepted to the right-fit college of your student's choice, the next chapter is most instructive.

"...there is a growing chorus of complaints from parents and students and some professors themselves---about excessively large classes, too many courses taught by grad students, and a lack of educational guidance for undergraduates."

Stanley N. Katz
"Does college need to be reformed?"
Slate Magazine website, 11/15/2005

How To Apply To College
One Chance To Make A First Good Impression.

Your student can have the decisive advantage in the application process, which means edging out competing students who have the same or slightly better grades.

This chapter will give you valuable tips on what to look for in the process, information that will not be illustrated for you by the colleges, guidance counselors, the Princeton Review, or by any college information night at your local high school. The positive by-product of this process will be a more mature student who has increased knowledge of who he is and what he values.

The Common Application is becoming more popular with schools because it asks questions which are "common" to all schools. Plus, students prefer the Common App because it relieves the stress of writing multiple essays for each school when they can write one essay and be done with it. When a college gives you a choice of using their own or the Common App, go with the Common App. Plus, because nearly all applications are done online, they prompt you for missing information. In other words, you will be assured to complete the application, which allows you an easier way to apply to a lot more schools.

Some schools will have their own questions, otherwise known as Supplements. Their purpose is to personalize the school that wants to ask specific questions, such as one college's request to get a Peer Review. You may have to write a short-answer essay, or the school could ask a simple question, such as, "What other colleges are you applying to?" Be sure to list your college choices alphabetically, not in order of choice.

Caution: you need to be accurate. The prompts can't tell you that you've entered the wrong social security number or a wrong birth date. Be very careful to check and recheck your information. Have another family member check your entries before submission.

The bottom line: if you're an admissions officer who reads thousands of applications, you're going to be very impressed with a student who does it correctly. For example, many essays are filled with spelling mistakes and grammatical errors, which demonstrate to the reader that the student didn't care about getting it right. How can a student be so lax and a parent too busy to check the student's entries before clicking SUBMIT? By having a perfectly spelled essay means giving yourself an edge in getting accepted. How hard is that? And if you're the admissions officer who's deciding on a perfectly done application, you've discovered a no-brainer: you're going to give this student an advantage over the student who didn't take the time to care about the "look" of the application.

What's the real impression you want to create? That you've already learned some great life-lessons most high school seniors haven't: that you go to great lengths to present yourself well, and that your work reflects attentiveness to and correctness of detail, which schools appreciate and rarely see. In short, you've set a standard by which all other applications are judged. You're ahead of your competition by filling out a application correctly.

Follow directions with extreme care. For example, a college's own application may ask you for the name of your county only to discover that "USA" was entered. It's a careless mistake. If you're near death in a hospital, you could be injected with the wrong drug because a nurse didn't take the time to read your chart carefully. Not paying attention to a little detail can kill. Since no college *needs* you, you can easily kill your chances of being accepted.

Theme The carefully done application makes the admissions person curious to see what else is special about your student. That "what else" should be a theme, a golden thread that weaves itself into every component of the application process: it's the student's passion, real interests - what makes the student unique. For example, a girl who is politically active in her community demonstrates the theme of politics; a boy who's an avid soccer player will have the theme of sports; a student who plays a piano will demonstrate a music theme. A theme makes it easy for the admissions officer to summarize the student for a fast or easier decision: "This young woman's going to be our state's youngest senator!," or, "This student will be a great addition to our school's soccer team!," or, "This kid's the next Elton John!"

Since schools are looking for a well-rounded student body instead of a well-rounded student, the student with a theme makes it easy for the admissions officer to decide how the student fits in and contributes to the college community.

Essay This is a huge opportunity for students to express their passion, or a strong interest in *something*, and what they've learned with their theme - expressed in a way that demonstrates good writing ability. Many schools give more weight to an essay than to an interview or class rank. The reason is two-fold: (1) with the increasing volume of applications flooding colleges each year, there's little or no time for interviews; and (2) an essay becomes your only personal communication about your theme. Imagine a 17-year-old political junkie, Thomas Jefferson, who submits an idea for starting a country with this title on his one-page essay: "Declaration of Independence." Would anyone have cared that young Tommy didn't show up for an interview? His theme? Politics. Apply to colleges with this single focus: write an essay to illustrate your theme so the reader gets a very good sense of who you are. Make it personal and persuasive.

Admission people know that as many as 70% of the applicants they accept won't show up in September. When they see another Uncle-Bob-Was-My-Inspiration essay, after a well-practiced yawn, they're not enthusiastic. Which begs the question: how do you convince the admissions committee that you want to attend their school and make them decide in your favor? Simply make the case that their school will make it easier to continue the pursuit of your interests.

Most schools allow you to pick your topic, and after writing your theme essay, answer the fantasy question that every admissions officer wants answered: *Why do you want to come to our school?* This *additional essay* should be submitted to illustrate strong evidence that you thoroughly researched the school, and why it matches what you want in a college. A Temple University official advised: "...a borderline candidate has a better chance at admission if they write a genuine essay that outlines precisely why they want and need to be admitted."

By contrast, avoid controversial subjects and boyfriend/girlfriend breakups. Moreover, since I know of no jars of valium cookies in any admissions office, stay away from the 4 "D" subjects: Death, Disease, Divorce, and Disorder (eating or drug). Rather than impress, they depress. Furthermore, don't write about trips, sports injuries, or your version of the Hail Mary pass. Most of all, don't fake it: colleges are very good at spotting fibs and exaggerations in an essay. And, please, NEVER use these two words together: "For me..." In short, be honest and don't try to impress. You'll impress by being honest.

Because I choose to assume the essay reader grew up watching Sesame Street with a certified attention span of 30 seconds, make certain your opening sentence is your most powerful - to get the reader's immediate attention. Hold that attention with a personal experience and give meaning to it with an insightful last sentence. For example, instead of concluding with, "I learned life skills," you should write, "The experience taught me the value of goals and the persistency required to achieve them." Give the reader a powerful last impression. Make it *Easy Decision* time: make the admissions office want you. When it comes to another student having the same or slightly better grades, but has a sloppy application and an off-limits essay, admission people have a long-standing affection for no-brainers. You win. You're in.

Biggest Mistake It's sending your essay to a school with another college's name in it. "I can't even begin to count the essays that I've read," complained one admissions officer, "that say 'and this is why I want to attend Carnegie Mellon University' [when the essay mentions another school's name].' Small details like that do make a difference. We don't care that you are applying elsewhere -- most students apply to more than one place -- but we do care that you couldn't take the time to change it to the correct university. Pay careful attention to the small details."

Write your essay in Microsoft Word (or any other word processing application), spell-check it, and save the final version as a plain text file to make it easy for you to easily copy and paste it into the online application.

Letters Of Recommendation (LOR) Recommendation letters have a way of perpetuating sameness, making the student look like everyone else. Nothing stands out. Predictable generalizations, standard clichés and pious platitudes inoculate the reader from taking such bland letters seriously. If you can, here's what you do: *no later than late spring of the junior year,* ask 2 teachers to write personal anecdotes that use your theme as the platform on which to illustrate who you are. For example, if the student's theme is sports, the writer can say: "Playing soccer has taught this student a persistency and dedication that he brings to every project he's assigned in the classroom." On its Common Application Supplement for the class of 2017, Dartmouth College states: "Specific anecdotes are much more helpful than general observations." In other words, sameness is a killer. Some colleges will place more value on these letters, suggesting that an adult can offer a better picture of the student's abilities and performance. Always call the college and ask *from whom* they require LORs. Before the letters are written, request that you receive a copy of each letter just before graduation: not only will you get to see what was said of you, but it will suggest to the writer that any negative comment will be viewed as the reason you were rejected by a college. No teacher will be foolish enough to write a negative comment only later to face a parent's flaming blow-back.

Resume Otherwise known as the "Activities Chart," it should be on one page, and it should read like a supplement to the application. Structure it so that the student's favorite activities and clubs are listed first to illustrate theme - what's most important to the student, rather than a chronology that reads like a sanitized airline schedule. When possible I have each of my students conclude their resumes with a line that gets a lot of laughs for its upbeat and positive zing, such as, "I've lived with the same parents all my life." Be sure to write a 3-4 line statement about the best thing you did in high school, and then highlight it with a yellow highlighter. No one in the admissions office will believe that the student did the highlighting. It may be assumed that somebody in the admissions office did the highlighting so that the reader wouldn't miss the best part. It's a creative way to "cheat" on your resume. Colleges also love newspaper clippings about a student, which you can attach to the resume. See *The Ultimate Admission Strategy* near the end of this book.

Interview Imagine ending an interview with a student who hands you a business card. The student's behaving on the same level of maturity as you. It's a huge plus for the student. Big edge. UnSame. Chances are excellent that you won't forget the student with the business card, and like a Christmas card you received with a photo, you're not likely to throw it away any time soon. A student should ask for interviews even where they're not required. Imagine the positive impression you make by *not* using these two words: "like" and "stuff." Making a good impression goes a long way toward getting an admissions officer to fight for you, as well as show the admissions people just how interested you are in their school. You would be among the few who the admissions people have seen and presumably like. Your objective is to stand apart from the rest, to get noticed and be remembered. Your application will be one of the few with a real face attached to it. It's easier to reject a piece of paper than a real person. Go for the interview at every opportunity.

The business card should have this information: name, town, State and email address, and without a phone number; no phone number communicates the easiest way to be reached. And at the top of the card should be the student's theme creatively expressed, such as, *"Piano Player - The Next Elton John!"* If your student has no special talent, then list good SAT scores, your large quantity of community service hours, or your best award - anything that reflects your theme. If you think of absolutely nothing to say, consider these words under your name, "Astonishingly Ordinary." Paper clip a card to all paperwork submissions. Goal? To stand out and apart from everyone else. Hand out your card to everyone in the admissions office and at college fairs. Be remembered in order to be admitted.

After returning home, only the student should write a "Thank You" card to the admission director. Resist stating the standard, "It was great visiting you and seeing your lovely campus." Write something of substance that shows you put some thought into it: "I stopped by the science department, and had a good conversation with..." Follow this procedure after the letter of acceptance arrives. This is a courtesy that should become a habit.

To be an *ideal* applicant is more likely to happen if a relationship has been established before the admission decision. To show real maturity and "ownership" of the admissions process, the student - *never* the parent - should be in contact by email with one good question at a time. Several contacts (*always* with the same person) will demonstrate a high...

Interest Level Most colleges are like an anxious teenage boy before the prom: he dreams of getting a bunch of calls from the girl of his dreams, and then he wants to be told he's been chosen as the one-and-only. Some colleges will print out a student's numerous emails and place them in a file to track interest; quantity can be quality. On the other hand many large colleges will openly tell you that they don't care about your interest level in their school. That's because they don't want 30,000 applicants calling every week to declare their undying love. But the human factor of your one-on-one communication with someone in the admissions office can still influence their decision about your application. Only 5% of incoming calls to an admissions office are from students. One admission counselor told me that she wants to scream after hanging up with a parent: "Have your son or daughter call me!"

In short, the information you've read so far guarantees your student an edge in being admitted. With all colleges watching, this is your American Idol moment. You want an admissions person to be your champion to increase your chances for acceptance. This is your *one and only chance* to be admitted.

Since schools spend millions to look gorgeous to prospective students, the suggestions here will make your student look like a million bucks to the schools. The college admission process begins as a courtship, and both players must look very appealing to the other. Students who make the effort to look and act attractive will catch the eye of a school that pursues what it assumes to be a solid match.

As other students will have similar grades and similar test scores - sameness - only your student will have a power presentation with a theme, an error-free application, a convincing essay, a highlighted resume, and evidence of courtesy and maturity. This "right of passage" for your student is happily accomplished.

Be sure your application is mailed *before anything else* because it's the "bulletin board" on which all your other supporting materials are pinned.

"It's all too easy for some students and faculty members to settle into a pattern of behavior that looks like an unspoken 'non-aggression treaty,' in which professors don't ask much of students and the students don't expect much from their professors (as long as they get A's and B's)."

John Merrow
President of Learning Matters, Inc
and co-editor of Declining by Degrees

Safety Schools
Harder To Enter

Approximately 20% of all applicants to so-called safety schools like Lamar Univ (TX) and Bridgewater State University (MA) are denied admission, and nearly 25% at Humboldt State Univ (CA) and 30% at St. Leo Univ (FL) are also denied. These are colleges whose minimum SAT scores start in the gutter 400s. Besides rejecting you for poor grades, you could have impressive grades and skills, and not fit the college's quest for more students from poor families, rich families, white families, black families, or albino Greek dwarf families from Long Island. You don't have to apply to a reach school to be rejected. On the other hand, an excellent student may find the admissions process less stressful and easier to handle if my instruction is followed in section, *The Math Of Admission.*

When more than 1,000 applying valedictorians are rejected by Harvard every year, or when 93% of the applicants to Yale are rejected, they go to their 2nd or 3rd choice schools. This hinders those less-than-superior students who were also hoping to get into their first choices. In turn, these students frustrate those who were planning on going to their match or safety schools. The pecking order is very selective, not to mention that 30% more high school grads are headed for college than 10 years ago. Ironically, the best students are most likely to experience the highest rejection rates by the most selective schools. Anyone who claims their kid will get into the college of their choice is walking on the thin ice of expectations.

Many students and parents must change their attitudes and perspectives. But how?

1. Challenge yourself: Taking unchallenging courses to get a bunch of A's doesn't always work. Colleges look for A's, B's and C's in Advance Placement (AP) for evidence that a student can handle challenges in college. Kathy Murphy, Director of Admissions of Assumption College (Worcester, MA), sums it up: "We are looking for students who will succeed." See section, *Admissions 101*, #1.

2. Prepare for college acceptance. High school is a time for nuts-and-bolts planning for your student's future. In a word, start no later than the 9th grade. Keep in touch often with several college admissions offices. To verify your interest in the college, many private colleges maintain databases to track how many times you make contact. Find excuses to *call* each college often with one question, the answer to which cannot be found on the college's website, such as, "Will this professor be teaching this particular course next fall?" In light of the Virginia Tech massacre, they may be surprised that you didn't ask about the school's safety record (Get it from the *campus police*, not the town police). Follow-up visits are a must. One of my students became a fixture with an admissions office. She played the college game like a champion and won. See section, ***Before The Junior Year.***

3. Community service Most want evidence your child doesn't act as if "It's all about me!" Have someone verify in writing all those community service hours. My clients with 9th graders have a goal of 500 hours in community service. It's not overkill, it's quantity that signals quality, that is, a quality person who makes time for others' needs and concerns, not just their own. Create your own project; stick with it while demonstrating passion and leadership, and colleges will be impressed. Get great ideas for your project by going to www.dosomething.org. Of the 26,208 hours you'll breathe over 3 years, 500 hours is only 1.9% of all that time. Anyone can prove they got an A, but not anyone can prove they became a better person. See section, ***Admissions 101***, #6.

4. Hire a private tutor to prepare for SATs and the ACT. The benefits far outweigh the cost, but many parents will nickel-and-dime their kids toward college, ignoring that every advantage for acceptance is needed. See section, ***SAT & ACT.***

5. Get a summer job. Never allow your student to work at a law firm. Colleges are repelled by gofers; however, they're impressed that your student developed a plan to make a small company run more efficiently. Nobody cares that the summer boss didn't adopt the plan, but that the student took the initiative to develop one. An impressed summer employer is a solid source for a great letter of recommendation. Ideally, get a job that's in sync with your passion or career goals. If you want to be a journalist, for example, offer to work for free at a media outlet. This will illustrate that your focus is on what you can learn, not on what you can earn. If you love soccer, find a way to be a soccer coach (or assistant coach) during the summer. The possibilities are limitless.

Private Colleges For Less
This Is No Rumor

Let's say your student applies to 2 colleges, one private and one state. The private costs $60,000 a year, and the state is $20,000 a year. So far, it's an easy choice - the state school.

Let's say your expected family contribution (EFC) is $20,000, the amount the Dept of Education has decided you can afford to pay out of your own pocket. Because the private university is well-endowed with lots of undesignated money, many end up giving you enough financial aid to cover all expenses above $20,000. All you pay out-of-pocket to send your child to a $60,000/year school is $20,000. Not even Dow Jones himself would give you this kind of return.

Unfortunately, a state school in the Northeast, which can be $23,000/yr (with room and board), does NOT have a lot of financial aid to give, and all they offer you is, say, $5,500 in a Stafford loan. Which means you still end up paying the full $23,000. The $60,000/yr school, which offered to cover all expenses over your $20,000 EFC, ends up being $3,000 less per year than the state school.

This scenario doesn't work as well with families whose AGI (adjusted gross income) is above $75,000.

The ideal financial aid scenario with a private college is to be an honor student from a poor family. Harvard, which can afford to do whatever its heart desires, likes to play with this destitution-with-talent scenario. On the other hand, some cynics would suggest correctly that the ideal situation for the college is awarding a bright student from a rich family because the college gets more money from the family. All the college needs to give this student is a minimum merit scholarship, just enough to bait the talented rich student to attend. That means the college doesn't have to dish out as much money as they would for a terrific student whose parents are poor. See section, *2 Dirty Secrets*.

Dumb Stuff
And Smart Stuff

Dumb: Private scholarship searches are not productive.
Here's how to punish your child creatively so it doesn't look like punishment: require him or her to look up scholarships on the web. After 3 hours, he may find a 100-dollar scholarship if you meet *all 3* of these conditions: you had an ancestor who died at the battle of Gettysburg, was left-handed, and fought for Texas. This long torturous exercise can prove to be futile if s/he doesn't know where to look. I suggest you look at these two sources: FinAid.org and then Google the name "Monica Matthews": she's the lady who wrote a small book describing in detail exactly how she got over $100,000 in scholarship money for her son.

Dumb: Most parents making over $100,000 per year don't qualify for financial aid.
Bill Gates qualifies for financial aid. You do too, no matter what your income. He can get a government-sponsored parent PLUS Loan from any number of banks. So can you. Unfortunately most parents give up before they even start, and assume they won't be eligible. In my former life, this mistake cost me over $50,000. If you fall into the category of living large (you make the big bucks), make sure you apply because everybody's eligible.

Dumb: Financial aid is given only to athletes, minorities, and academic superstars.
These categories do get preference, but "need-based" financial aid is awarded based solely on financial need, which is calculated by taking a school's cost of attendance (COA) and subtracting the expected family contribution (EFC). That's the minimum amount the government says you can afford to pay, based on parent and student income, assets and several other factors. Whatever is left over after you subtract these two numbers is your "financial need," or maximum eligibility for financial aid at a particular school. This has nothing to do with a student's ethnic background, athletic ability, or grades. It's based on this formula:

> COA (Cost Of Attendance)
> <u>- EFC (Expected Family Contribution)</u>
> = Your Financial Need

Dumb: Pay no attention to how your student compares to a prospective school's profile.

To increase your chances of getting the best possible financial aid package, it's imperative that you pick schools where your child places in the top 20% of the incoming freshman class with respect to their GPA and SAT/ACT scores. Although most schools give financial aid based on your calculation of "need," they will give preferential packaging (i.e., more FREE money, less loans) to students who place in the top 20% of the incoming class. They do this to attract better students to their school. That's why talented children of millionaires can get thousands of free dollars. Some schools will practically beg your kid to come to their school by giving you more FREE money if, for example, his/her SAT scores are better than the school's average. This will motivate the college to bribe your student to attend. In this college admission game, it's perfectly legal for your student to take a bribe.

Dumb: All schools give the same amounts of money.

Many schools receive a lot of donations from alumni and corporations, and have more money to meet most or all of a student's financial need. Other schools, such as state universities, get little or no private funds, and rely solely on state and federal funds to help fill a student's need. These schools leave students short and give them less money than they are eligible to receive. It can actually end up costing you more to send your child to a state school if it doesn't have the money to meet your need. See section, *Private Colleges For Less*.

Know each school's profile of giving money before you ever apply so you're not blown away when you get a small financial aid package from your child's top choice. Preparation will produce success. Go to www.collegeboard.com for what colleges report as their true average aid packages. The figures can be misleading, but they're starting points. Just because a college states that it meets 80% of your financial need doesn't mean they can't or won't give you more. They assume you don't know how the college game is played, and you'll accept any offer that comes close to the published figure. You can work some magic if you see section, *After The Award Letter*.

"If you happen to be applying," concludes SmartMoney.com, "when the school is under siege from needy students, your chances of receiving a good package are much lower. The lesson: Apply as early as possible." See section, *EarlyEarlyEarlyEarlyEarly*.

Dumb: There's no difference between "includable assets" and "non-includable assets" for purposes of qualifying for financial aid.

Certain assets are included in the financial aid formulas, which are the legal equivalent to the tax code. For example, cash, savings accounts, CDs, 529 plans, trusts, stocks, bonds, and other real estate are all "includable" and asked about on the FAFSA, the federal financial aid form; however, it does not ask about the value of three other financial vehicles. Put available assets into any of these three non-includable areas to qualify for more aid: (1) retirement plans, (2) annuities, or (3) cash-value life insurance policies. One of these hidden money safe-havens, a life insurance policy known as a modified endowment contract (MEC), offers a proven and creative way to finance a college education that is hardly known to most financial experts. It's not even mentioned on the most popular website on financial aid - FinAid.org. CAUTION: a MEC is like a moving target with moving circles: it can be very complicated. And if you're not careful with selecting a financial expert who knows the ins and outs of this financial vehicle, don't bother.

Dumb: It doesn't matter where your money is.

Where you keep your money could mean the difference between getting $10,000 in financial aid and getting nothing. For example, money in the child's name is penalized nearly four times more than money in the parent's name, or a minimum of 20% versus 5.6 percent. Or, money in an UGMA or 529 savings plan can count against you as much as 20% to 100 percent. If you don't know how to position your money legally for the purpose of getting more financial aid, you could end up losing thousands of dollars each year.

Dumb: Accountants can fill out financial aid forms.

CPAs and tax preparers are experts at tax planning and preparation, not *financial aid* planning. For example, a CPA might suggest you put some or all of your assets in your child's name. While this advice can help you save on taxes, it will cause you to lose on financial aid. Also, tax preparers are not trained to fill out financial aid forms. We have seen many cases where they unknowingly filled out these forms incorrectly (i.e., omitting social security numbers, or placing the parent's assets in the wrong space), and these minor mistakes will bump your financial aid forms and cost you tons of cash. If this happens, you will have to re-submit these forms, and you may end up losing thousands in financial aid since colleges award their own aid on a first-come, first-served basis. See section, *FAFSA FUMBLE.*

Dumb: Planning is no necessity.
To legally set up your assets so you can maximize your eligibility for financial aid, reposition them *by Dec 31st of the student's sophomore year.* Why? So that the tax return for the next year (examined by the colleges) has no record of the earnings on the sale of stocks, bonds, CDs, mutual funds - capital gains. Even if you're late, move the money anyway and consider *not* filling out a FAFSA form for the first college year: you now have time to reposition assets, and then fill out the FAFSA in the 2nd year when the assets will be hidden (of course, you forego any federal aid in the first year by not submitting a FAFSA). Certain other funds, such as 529s, UTMAs and UGMAs, could be repositioned in the senior year of high school, but timing is everything. Before you make any moves, call me and I'll suggest what to do in *your* specific circumstance. As you're reading this, chances are good you're already late.

The longer you wait and the closer it gets to your child's senior year, the tougher it gets to set up your financial situation without creating a "red flag" for the colleges and universities. It's also important to know your EFC (Expected Family Contribution) so you can start planning for it. Know which schools can give you the best packages before you start visiting and applying to them. If you haven't started planning, see section, *What You Absolutely Must Do Right Now* toward the end of this book.

Dumb: Take the SAT/ACT test twice, but no more.
I once criticized a local high school's guidance office for giving parents some very bad advice on the frequency of taking the SATs, and as a consequence I became toxic dog meat at two other area high schools - ready for this? - for my *lack of support for public education.* My point: take the SATs as often as you want, or at least twice *after you've been tutored privately.* Chances are very good that your scores will improve. Typical of what college admissions people think of frequency: "Be sure to take the SAT or ACT at least three times," says Paul Cukanna of Duquesne University. "In the eye of an admission officer, repeated SAT tests indicate motivation rather than desperation."

Dumb. Really Dumb: **Do it yourself and save.**
It amazes me that people will readily use a doctor when they get sick, an accountant at tax time, a lawyer when they get sued, but when they're expected to spend $23,000 to $69,000 per year for college, parents want to save themselves a few bucks and do the

admissions and financial aid processes themselves. Unless you've spent the last 15 years of your life doing it, there's no way you're going to know how to get the "edge" in admissions and the maximum amount of money from each school. So who you gonna call? Right...you can access me for free at 1-508-520-6642.

"The unnecessarily complex forms can be confusing... Students should be more challenged by their homework in college than their paperwork to receive student aid. If a student is able to fill out the form as it exists today, I don't think they should have to go to college – they should go straight to grad school."

Rahm Emanuel
Mayor of Chicago

FAFSA FUMBLE
How It Works

The FAFSA (Free Application for Federal Student Aid) form is what you must fill out in order to get *any* need or non-need financial aid, such as a subsidized Stafford loan for the need, or an unsubsidized Stafford for the non-need. It's easy to fill out: with over 100 questions it comes complete with instructions, and if you need a professional to help you, you can always call the FAFSA toll-free phone number (800-433-3243) and someone will take all the time you need to fill our your FAFSA correctly.

Watch out for your own mistakes. One of the worst is placing your retirement monies on the line marked "investments." One of my clients, whose daughter was a college senior when we first met, designated an IRA rollover worth $200,000 as an "investment." This was a knife-in-your-gut mistake. Before I met the client, she had placed that same figure on that line for 3 years in a row. Here's the damage she did: the school saw $200,000 and multiplied it by 5.6% *each year!* That meant that the school happily penalized the student by $11,200 per year X 3 years. The daughter lost $33,600 in financial aid because mother didn't read correctly Worksheet B of the FAFSA form. Until I showed up, she didn't have a clue that she had lost all that money in financial aid. This client was an accountant.

Another mistake is to indicate that your child has, for example, $900 in a savings account by answering question #43, which pertains to the student:

> **"As of today, what is your...total current balance**
> **of cash, savings, and checking accounts?"**

Very mechanically and honestly you entered, "$900." That was easy, but you took the bait and walked into a trap that will be a signal to all colleges to get out their party hats and begin celebrating their gain.

Here's what you did: you told the colleges that they can penalize your child for $180 in financial aid for each year the money remains in the child's bank account. That's because the federal aid rules (the legal equivalent to the tax code) allow colleges to penalize student assets by at least 20% versus 5.6% of parent assets. The thinking at colleges goes like this: if the child has $900, then the child can use $180 (20% of $900) to help pay for education. That means the college will deduct $180 from their financial aid package, a deduction you will never notice. That's the welcome gain you just gave the college. They score in this part of the game.

Schools won't be calling you in a spasmodic fit of generosity to suggest that you transfer that $900 into the parent's account, before you file the FAFSA, so they can penalize it at only 5.6%, or $50. You can easily make the transfer the day before you sign the FAFSA, and it's perfectly legal if it's taken out of your child's savings account and put into your account. Look again at the key phrase of Question 43: "As of today..." Be sure it was *yesterday* you made the winning move of transferring the money. You score in this part of the game. And you thought politicians were the only people who played silly shell games.

If your student owns custodial accounts, CDs, EE savings bonds, or mutual funds, the formula changes. You can't go by the "As of today..." time-frame. Ideally, remove these assets from the student's name before December 31st of the sophomore or junior years, depending on what school your student wants to attend. This is a rule that's not always enforced, but it's better to be safe than sorry if you meet a financial aid director who has a sharp eye on your finances. See section, *If Your Child Is A High School Junior...* item #4.

If the student will file a tax return because there were interest earnings and/or capital gains, in order to be "invisible" in the financial aid formulas, the money must be repositioned.

Colleges are in the business of confiscating your money, not to give you their money. If a single college ever calls you to suggest where to put that $900 so you can get more aid, tune in to the Weather Channel to watch this amazing announcement: "The depths of Hell are presently at freezing temperatures! It's gone viral already."

An overwhelming number of FAFSA forms are submitted with errors or inconsistencies, which means yours may get kicked back so you can experience the purple agony of filling out your FAFSA all over again. The Department of Education knows that

(1) your attitude is already negative about filling out forms,
(2) you expect instant results in a fast-service culture, and
(3) you have no patience or time for filling out forms.
That's 3 strikes against you before you fumble with the FAFSA, not to mention *you're required to fill out a FAFSA every year in order to*

receive financial aid. For the process to work every year, your yearly punishment is required.

Plus, simple mistakes like omitting a single digit of a social security number, forgetting a middle initial, or neglecting to sign the form can actually bump a FAFSA back to you.

If this happens, you will have to resubmit it, which can take another 2-4 days before you can discover if you did it correctly the second time. Why would you even allow this possibility to exist when there's so much money at stake? My clients escape this nonsense by calling the FAFSA people directly to get help.

Since most financial aid is awarded on a first-come, first-served basis, submit your aid forms accurately within the first 2 weeks of January (or, as early as October starting in 2016), or hire someone who's done it hundreds of times. Otherwise, you take the chance of losing thousands of dollars in this entire process. The American Council on Education estimates that 1.8 million families don't fill out the FAFSA form. There's no gun to their heads, but they're not receiving any federal aid either.

Colleges have the right to send a copy of your tax return to the IRS. If the tax return you sent to the college doesn't match the tax return you sent to the IRS, you risk paying a $20,000 fine or spending a year in jail. The only reason to be fraudulent with your FAFSA is to look stunning in an orange jumpsuit.

"College websites illustrate the millions they spend on marketing their product, just as Mercedes, Rolex, and Calvin Klein do. A college's primary objective is to get your money, not give you theirs. They prefer to impress your student with a 'free' iPod whose cost is buried in your overly inflated tuition payments."

Paul Lloyd Hemphill

CSS Profile
The *Mother-In-Law Of All Forms*

After completing the FAFSA, you thought you were all done filling out the forms for financial aid. Along comes the equivalent of a blood-sucking mosquito attack called the CSS Profile. Courtesy of most private schools.

Where the FAFSA asks for one year of financial information, the CSS Profile will ask for 2 years, and then it will ask you to use your crystal ball to predict what you'll make next year. Real total: 3 years. Total questions: about 200. I'm not making this up.

The "privates" can ask you about the contents of your retirement plans, your kid sister's savings account, all real estate holdings, annuity amounts, the cash value of your life insurance, and your expenses. And get this: they don't care about your $15,000 credit card debt or a $30,000 debt in car payments.

If you were required to furnish all this financial information to a car dealer before buying a car, a publicity-seeking lawyer would happily file a lawsuit on your behalf knowing the story would be front-page news. Of course, the colleges would rev up their arrogance machinery to remind us clueless parents that they don't sell cars. Of course, how silly to think such a thing!

The only debt for which you get any credit from *private* colleges is home debt. So don't make those extra payments every month. The more equity you have, the less aid you'll receive. If you're mortgaged to the hilt, buy a bottle of champagne and pop that cork to celebrate! You'll qualify for a lot more aid than most parents. Conversely, if you have very little left on your mortgage, you'd better call the financial aid version of 911: yours truly.

If you own a business or you're self-employed, your accountant will be forced to fill out a Business/Farm Supplement. Naturally, he may not fill it out for free. If you're divorced or separated, a Non-Custodial profile will be generated, and that means the college will go after the non-custodial parent for tax returns, W2s - the works.

As if you're not already going nuts, many schools will ask you their "supplemental" questions. They can include everything from asking what cars you own, complete with model and year, to see if you own any late-model or "luxury" cars. And - brace yourself - they'll ask what religion you practice. Good God!

Here's the next gut kick: every school can send their own income Verification form (college version of an audit) with the same questions you answered on the FAFSA to make sure you didn't lie. They'll also ask for your tax return and W2 to see if they can catch you in a lie. No one ever told these people that trust is a beautiful thing. And you thought only your mother-in-law was distrustful.

There is one redeeming feature of the CSS Profile: it has a Special Circumstance section that allows you to explain why you need more aid due to circumstances over which you have no control. I've seen colleges award more aid because a client recently lost his job, became suddenly disabled, lost the house in a violent storm - anything that would suggest a valid hardship. When you write the statement, be dispassionate and factual. No emotion here, or else you could be ignored.

When you're filling out this form, be certain that the information matches what you filled out on the FAFSA (some colleges will request the CSS Profile be filled out before the FAFSA). If you make a single error, such as misplacing the wrong digit in a social security number, it could cause the entire process to slow down. You could be back to square one. Score one for the colleges.

The CSS Profile is the grand validation of the following: your punishment is always required, trust is truly non-existent, colleges are gladly in your face about your finances like no other entity on earth, and your mother-in-law is now looking like a gift from God.

SAT & ACT
Private Tutor = Higher Scores = More Aid

Have your child take the PSAT to discover weakness and strength. Take the SAT 3 or 4 times after the 9th grade. Retaking the test, says the College Board website, "increases his or her combined critical reading and mathematics scores by approximately 30 points." That's hardly impressive. There are free online workshops you can visit: www.sat.etestprep.com and www.revolutionprep.com. One-on-one coaching *before the senior year* is a gargantuan plus.

Higher scores are compulsory in an increasingly competitive environment. See section, **Admissions 101**, #3. They're also a great way to get more financial aid. Two examples:

1. A family's son missed out on an additional $6,000 per year - that's $24,000 over 4 years - of free money because he was only 10 points shy of the college's next higher SAT threshold for additional aid. His score was 1090 (excluding the writing portion), but an 1100 score would have won him the extra money. Hiring a tutor to improve the student's verbal skills would have been a no-brainer.

2. A family's daughter was tutored privately, and her SAT scores went from 2070 to 2250. She was accepted at a college whose SAT average was below 2250. Her scores, as the college saw them, raised the school's average, so the school saw this student as good window-dressing, that is, higher SAT-achieving students impress college-shopping parents. She was offered a scholarship for $12,000 per year - $48,000 in FREE money over 4 years. Hiring a private tutor at $200 per hour (read: Don't go cheap!) was an incredible investment.

Tip #1: When asked why he robbed banks, the infamous bank robber Willie Sutton said, "That's where the money is." A private school is where the money is. Apply to private, matching and safety schools for potentially more aid. These schools want better test-scoring students so that they can tell parents like you what a quality school they have for your mon--, er, little darling. These schools will bribe you with a more generous aid package.

Tip #2: Use higher SAT/ACT scores to apply to more selective schools which offer more aid. High test scores are no longer a distinguishing factor - they're required. But just in case those rejection letters come in from first-choices, there can be lots of gold in those March award letters from schools with less stringent standards who really want your student for the purpose of improving their own image. Both student and college are marketing to each other. When it comes to getting more financial aid, and because the college industrial complex is such a huge business, getting into college or getting more financial aid *begins with good marketing.*

Tip #3: Colleges like the ACT because it's better at measuring what you know. The SAT's national average score is 1,000 the ACT's national composite average is around 21.

Not all schools require SAT scores. A religious-affiliated college issued a self-serving press release, stating it will no longer require SAT scores for admission. When asked, "Why would a student submit standardized test scores if they don't have to?" Their answer: "A student might decide that his or her score gives a more complete picture of academic achievements and potential." Replace the word "student" with the word "college" and you have Truth in Advertising. So far, roughly 70% of applying students to such schools submit their SAT scores anyway. Talk about being competitive!

This school will use the SATs as the logical tie-breaker to award financial aid to highly competitive applicants.

Check this added whopper: "We have been concerned," says the college in justifying the requirement, "about the inherent racial and socioeconomic bias in standardized testing..." Cynics will be watching for this college to announce the rejection of its religious affiliation because of its church's "inherent bias against atheists in standardized tests of faith." It's a typical elitist college using feel-good Oprah babble in their press release.

If these non-SAT schools were honest and forthright, they would *require* that students NOT submit their test scores. For stealth purposes their hypocrisy is astounding. Marketing trumps truth.

For students who don't test well, consider a smaller school that places more emphasis on grades than SAT/ACT scores. On how to get higher test scores, see section, *If Your Child Is A High School Junior...* item #2.

A Self-Inflicted Injury
A High School's College Night

I don't wish this abuse on anyone - attending a high school's college information or financial aid night. To be fair, it's not a total waste of time because you'll experience, up close and personal, the brutality of truth. You'll witness an eager speaker delivering an unforgiving blizzard of details on how to fill out forms and other mind-numbing paperwork. This person just so happens to be - brace yourself - a financial aid officer from a college. It's the friendly fox lecturing the unsuspecting chickens. She'll use the offensive 4-letter word - LOAN - like a blunt instrument, swinging it without mercy for two punishing hours. Your local high school neglected to warn you that tonight marks the date of your first nervous breakdown.

Why would a college financial aid person even hint at a single legal way to get more money from their coffers that are found in this book? Would a banker give you his bank's access code so you could easily rob it? Part of the college's game is to keep you uninformed about the rules of the game and to get you to spend more of your money, not to give you theirs. And they love lecturing you on what loan-troths you can feed at in order to pay their overly inflated fees.

Here's a sample announcement from a high school's website on their financial aid night:

PARENT FORUM COLLEGE FINANCING SEMINAR An experienced financial aid professional will conduct the Seminar. Topics:

- · The college financial aid application process;
- · Completing the FAFSA;
- · Resources for scholarships and grants;
- · Determining financial aid eligibility;
- · Student loans, parent loans, and payment plans;
- · New resources for families

In sum, these nights are a lecture on the required paperwork and cost problems with *more debt as your solution*. In two hours, you will suffer perhaps the same mental anguish that prisoners receive in any two hours of a warden's lecture on how to clean toilets.

Never discussed at these high school aid nights are proven ways to pay for the bulk of college expenses. Never mentioned are the advantages of community colleges. God forbid! That would be discussing the competition, and in fairness to the speaker, we shouldn't expect a lecture on the competition. By the way, Bill Gates qualifies for financial aid, so "eligibility" - as suggested on the high school's website - is misleading and a non-issue.

Going to a high school's college or financial aid night is a self-inflicted injury in a near pity-party atmosphere.

Your local high school is a well-intentioned but unintended co-conspirator with the colleges in keeping parents ignorant of how to save money on skyrocketing college costs. Because I make a profit, I don't get invited to speak at high schools on the topic of financial aid. Yet the school will invite a college official to give a seminar on this subject, with a mouth fully engaged on how parents can get into more debt. No one even realizes the college official represents a business entity that is price-gouging the very parents the well-intentioned high school wants to help.

———————————

"Let's see if we can follow the [professor's] logic: Students don't read what they are assigned, so it becomes important to assign them less reading. Talk about a race to the bottom."

Naomi Schaefer Riley
Wall Street Journal, 8/25/2005

A Senior Moment
Colleges Can Use It Against You

Senior Moment summary: "I can coast to graduation."

Seniors shouldn't forget that the entire senior year is as important as the junior year. AP doesn't mean Automatically Privileged. Colleges are looking to see if the student is a slacker. It's their opportunity to withdraw admission (read: lose thousands of dollars in financial aid) if your student's grades are headed south.

Why would a student give a college an excuse to withdraw admission and lose a bunch of money? Is your senior taking time off from studying in the last semester? If so, prepare to give a bullet-proof reason. Colleges are watching with eagle eyes.

Be sure to warn your senior of the thousands of dollars that are at stake if they indulge their version of a Senior Moment, *getting caught up in entertaining distractions instead of focusing on good grades until graduation.* If your student isn't careful, lower 2nd semester grades can produce a financial aid disaster. Colleges can withdraw scholarships thereby causing you to lose the original aid package with thousands of dollars evaporating into thin air.

Here are two typical warning notices from many colleges in their award letters: "Your admission and financial aid awards are dependent on your successful performance until graduation." Or, "We require you to submit your final high school transcript by July 1st." Your student's on notice; your senior's trap has been set.

If this warning condition is not included in the acceptance or award letter, is it possible the college is giving a pass to the student who's proven to be exceptional throughout high school? Call any admissions office and ask if they'll give a "pass" to your little Einstein in the last semester. Imagine hearing laughter as you wait for the answer. It's okay to have a Senior Moment when you're age 68, but not this kind at age eighteen.

Getting The Most Aid
Timing Is Everything

1. Apply to at least 10 colleges.

Apply to 2 types of schools: "safety" and "match" schools. You wouldn't buy a car if there's more than a 50% chance of it breaking down in a week. Yet adults will advise students to apply to "reach" schools with a less than 20% chance of acceptance. The best Ivy candidates have as much as a 90% rejection rate. Don't lower standards, but be practical. If there's a good chance of getting into a reach school, and aid doesn't matter, go for it. Apply to 8 or 9 match schools where you fit the college's profile with a 60%-80% chance of admission. Then apply to 2 to 4 safety schools that are most likely to accept you. You also increase your chances of getting more aid on appeal at these schools since, for example, matching schools will be more receptive to an appeal when they know they're competing with a school in the same league. If a matching school is competing with a better aid offer from a safety school, your appeal will need a respirator.

By applying to at least 10 schools you will greatly increase your ability to appeal financial aid packages; you'll be able to play one school's offer against another's. Colleges find themselves faced with more *accepted* students not showing up in September because increasingly more students are applying to more than 6 or 8 colleges. Which is all my fault. Plus, with only a few college choices needed to complete Step Six of your FASFA form, each school assumes you're applying to lots of other schools, and that you don't yet believe their school to be the one-and-only hallowed institution worth your overly committed, wildly enthusiastic and on-your-knees consideration.

Repeat this technique in the following years by listing 2 cheaper schools in Step Six of the FAFSA. Why? Give the college the impression that your student is transferring, which they'll interpret as an unintentional threat to slaughter their most sacred cow: their retention rate (read: income). A college will be forced to consider giving you more aid next year, and likely in the form of grants instead of loans. Always be asking for aid.

If you receive a financial aid package that's less than the year before, ask the college before the next semester to send your student's freshman or sophomore transcript to 2 other schools. If your tuition costs are, say, $45,000 a year at College XYZ, and your student drops out, the school stands to lose over $130,000 over the next 3 years. It's perfectly legal strategy to frighten extra aid out of colleges since they automatically frighten extra money out of you each year. Fair is fair. The potential loss in revenues to the college sounds off all kinds of alarms. Rule of thumb: always play hardball. This is a very expensive game where the college's objective is to get as much of your money without giving you any of theirs. In sum, adopt their greedy mind-set.

2. Price your home.

Don't over-estimate the value of your home. For purposes of financial aid, with exceptions like Harvard, Princeton, Emory and Carnegie Mellon, most private colleges count against you the equity in your home. And except for the University of Michigan at Ann Arbor and the University of North Carolina at Chapel Hill, state schools don't care. You can use this special formula, The Housing Index Multiplier, which can be found on the web:

http://www.finaid.org

This is based on your home's original purchase price and the year you bought it. When you see the final minimum calculation, use this figure on the CSS Profile (required by most private colleges, but not required by state schools). **Caution:** many colleges are dropping the Index Multiplier as the standard yardstick to determine your home equity, and instead are using real estate websites to determine your "fair market value." Colleges are good at stretching yardsticks.

The true *market* value of your home, or what your town's tax assessor says it's worth, is totally irrelevant in the college money game. Find out what your "multiplier" is and use this value for your home when applying to colleges that require the CSS Profile. But be prepared for the college to come back with what they regard as "fair market value." The difference could be enormous. There are 28 "elite" schools that count the market value of your house at 1.2 times your income as an available asset *regardless of your equity*. If you have a bright student and a middle-class income, you will want to know the names of these colleges. They can be found in the back of this book under **Article Sources**, in section, **Getting The Most Aid**.

3. Lower out-of-pocket costs now.

Assets in the wrong locations will damage your chances of getting all the money to which you are entitled. For example, never put or keep more than $67 (use any figure under $100 but over $50 - it just looks credible) in your student's name if you already qualify for need-based aid; the same goes for siblings when filling out the CSS Profile (sibling assets are not required on the FAFSA). Be sure both your student and siblings are asset-poor. Student assets in UGMA or UTMA accounts need to be repositioned very carefully. Repositioning gifted money that's already in a child's name requires a simple but little-known legal mechanism that's exercised by transferring the funds into a modified endowment contract (MEC) where the UGMA/UTMA purchases the MEC. It's not an automatic, slam-dunk move, and you want to exercise a boatload of caution on how you do it. It's complicated and only an astute financial expert ought to assist you in this exercise.

4. Submit financial aid forms on time.
The earliest date you can file the Free Application For Federal Student Aid (FAFSA) is Jan 1 (as early as October beginning in 2016); however, many private schools will ask you to fill out the CSS Profile, with dates that could be before January. Different schools have different deadlines for this form, which is usually in February. Caution: Never miss a deadline.

5. Ignore guidance counselors.
Most high school guidance counselors tell parents to simply fill out the forms. End of story. Experienced guidance counselors are good at helping your student get into college based on personal relationships they've established with many college admission directors. But this kind of counselor, with increasing numbers of students and responsibilities that have nothing to do with college admissions, is becoming less available, particularly in public schools. For the most part, these counselors have too much on their plates, with national student-to-counselor ratios averaging 457:1 at public high schools and 241:1 at private high schools. A 500:1 ratio is not unusual.

Whenever physical paperwork of any kind is sent to a college, send it by Delivery Confirmation Receipt. Demand from the high school guidance office that it provide you evidence of having sent your child's paperwork, particularly their transcript and teachers' letters of recommendations (you will send the applications, essays and resumes yourself by electronic of Priority Mail, and notify the College Board where to send the SAT scores). After each piece of mail goes out, the student should follow up one week later with a phone call to each college to verify that the paperwork was received.

This could make you a world-class pain in the posteriors of some guidance counselors, but why would you trust them with the small details that could sink your child's future? Give the guidance office several pre-addressed Priority Mail envelopes with the postage already affixed. Immediately after Labor Day of your student's senior year, have an understanding, without subtlety, of *what you expect* from the high school guidance office.

One of my clients had a son at a parochial school with a strict policy on handling all the paperwork for college. The school was suggesting that their son's future would be placed in the hands of a guidance counselor who barely knew the student and was managing the paperwork for more than 50 other students. (That's when you know the red flag of Murphy's Law is waving triumphantly: if something will go wrong, it will.) I advised the client to tell the school where they could stick their policy (of course, in some round file), and that the parent had her own policy that would allow the school to send out only the transcript and letters of recommendation. In short, some high school guidance offices may object to what you're asking, but it's *your* policy about *your* child that they must honor. Period.

Play hardball with these kinds of stubborn guidance offices because this is your child's future at stake, and no school's policy that keeps you out of the loop should be respected. I've seen students not get into the college of their choice because of a distracted or uncommitted guidance counselor who missed a college's deadline, or forgot to send the student's transcript. Such unconscionable possibilities should be addressed from the start of the admission process. See **Guidance Counselors** toward the end of this book.

College aid officers, or high school guidance counselors, may offer to help you apply for financial aid. Don't accept the offer. Going to a college financial aid officer is like going to the IRS for help to reduce your taxes, and colleges will direct you to where you can get more loans. With the exception of merit scholarships, the schools have no interest in teaching you how to get free money from them. But you already knew this, right?

Most CPAs and nearly all financial planners are equally inept in the area of college financial aid. And people who are in the business of college financial aid haven't a clue about the admissions process and how integral it is to obtaining financial aid.

EarlyEarlyEarlyEarlyEarly
Good & Bad

Early Action (EA) A student should apply EA to *matching* and *safety* schools, where GPA and test scores match or exceed the school's averages, and apply later to 1 or 2 *reach* schools as part of the Regular Decision (RD) pool. The very best students apply EA at the schools that have it, thereby decreasing your chances for acceptance and merit aid if you're not at least a matching student. The earlier you get noticed at your match and safety schools, when you're not part of the huge herd of applicants who are pulling their hair out later, the more you can max your chances, learn your fate sooner, reduce lots of stress, and increase your chances for merit aid if you're in the top 20% of incoming students. By definition, *reach* schools are unlikely to award you any merit aid.

For an Early Action decision, apply between mid-September and mid-October and obtain a decision in December. There's no obligation to attend any of the schools which accept you. This allows you to apply to several colleges without submitting the dreaded aid forms until January. If you follow my advice on the right way to apply to college (See section, **How To Apply To College**), not only will your thematic paperwork create the standard by which all other applications will be judged, but your chances for acceptance at the college of your choice will increase substantially.

Early Read The Academic Dean of Poker loves this one. Some colleges will offer to calculate your EFC (Expected Family Contribution), that is, look at your financial picture and tell you what you must spend and what your aid package will look like. The "dealer" wants to see your hand before you play it. Never give a college a hint of what you're holding because this could be the most expensive hand you'll ever play.

Early Admission This is for the brightest student. Apply at the beginning of the junior year, assuming that all requirements for high school are already completed. Colleges will compete to have bragging rights for a student of this quality. Full scholarships are not unusual. There's no requirement to attend the school once you're accepted.

Early Notification This one crawls out from under the slime. The college wants you to commit to their financial aid package well before their usual deadline, which is May 1. It looks like the infomercial that screams, "This offer is good only for the next 15 minutes!" Keep the process on your terms: wait and weigh all offers.

Early Decision (ED) This is a college's gun-to-your-head favorite. You'll be forced to sign a binding contract committing your student to that school once s/he's accepted. This makes you a hostage to whatever aid package they offer, on their terms and on their notification schedule. Not only do they hold the cards in this game, but you're giving them the entire deck to stack against you. "Early Decision is a mess," says David Hawsey, Vice President for Enrollment at Albion College, Michigan, "and students are the ones who suffer."

The dirty little secret is that Early Decision favors the student of a wealthy parent.

Here's the real question: Why would you give any college the slightest game advantage over you when so much money is at stake? We can think of only two reasons: (1) you make over $200,000 a year and have too many assets to ever qualify for need-based aid, or (2) your daughter has threatened to marry the exterminator if she doesn't go the college of her dreams.

In short, Early Decision should be considered only if the student is adamant and committed to going to that school. Passion and commitment to that school is what every college is looking for - it's another edge in getting accepted. That's even if grades - and I hesitate to state this - are not quite what they should be.

"Applying early," claim the authors of *The Early Admissions Game*, "provides a significant admissions advantage, approximately equivalent to the effect of a jump of 100 points in SAT-1 score." This claim makes sense as another yardstick to help decide who gets in and who doesn't.

Pick A College
Curriculum And Fit Are Most Important

Most families start planning trips to visit one or more of the schools in which the student has an interest. This is how most students and families get to know each college campus, and determine if they would feel comfortable being a student there. To get a better idea of how current college students rate their own colleges, both parents and prospective students are going to college admissions blogs, if available, or to two popular websites: www.collegeprowler.com and www.crapcampus.com.

Reality Check #1 Travel from campus to campus to get a flavor of what kind of setting you find most comfortable. Once this physical comfort zone is established, it's time to discover if your GPA and test scores match a college's criteria for acceptance. The fastest way to find out is to go to collegeboard.com, look up the college's profile, and click on the section marked, **SAT©, ACT©, CLEP©.** You'll see the college's Middle 50% of First-Year Students, and that's when you discover you're a match, or not a match. If it's a reach school, don't waste your time; there are simply too many good match and safety schools that deserve your attention and where you're likely to get more aid (read: less debt after graduation).

Male applicants at most colleges may not have an advantage just because schools have a gender imbalance. For example, former all-women universities aren't running national ad campaigns to recruit more men. Yet those schools are quickly becoming a male's dream come true: two girls to every boy. See section, *The Cost Of Diversity*.

Here's the right way to look for colleges. Instead of blindly picking schools based on academic or sports standards, or because your friend or relative's son loves a particular college for its landscaping and parties, look at 5 important criteria:

(1) Does this college have the curriculum that ideally suits your student? If Princeton doesn't have what you're looking for, why apply there? Is it because you think a degree from a brand-name school will better your career prospects? Be careful. See section, *Ask Tough Questions,* question #2.

(2) Does your student qualify to get into this college? This is where you find out if your student fits the school's typical freshman class with similar grades and SAT/ACT scores. This would be a match school.

(3) Can this school meet your financial need by giving you more FREE money and fewer loans? Even a state school can cost you $20,000 or more per year when you include tuition, beer, books, beer, room, beer, board, beer, and other living expenses. A private university can now run you over (pun intended) $70,000 per year.

(4) My kid got into 3 schools, which she loves. Holy decision! Now what? Explore in depth what courses are being offered at each school. Talk to the career office and ask what support system is in place to help you get a job when you graduate. Compare schools: sit through 2 classes in which you have an interest and see how professors relate to students. Walk around the campus and ask students only 2 questions: (1) "What do you like about this school?," and (2) "What don't you like about this school?" Helicopter parents (hovering) should absolutely stay away. If you must be on campus during the visit, walk 5,280 feet behind your student so s/he's in tune with his or her gut feelings about the school's environment. Better yet, get off campus and take in a movie. Relax. In other words, get lost.

(5) Reality Check #2 Let's look at how the financial process works. Financial aid is awarded at most schools based on a calculation of a family's "financial need." Financial need is calculated by subtracting your EFC (Expected Family Contribution), which is the minimum amount you will be expected to pay at any school, from the COA (Cost of Attendance), which includes tuition, fees, books, room and board, travel, and chemically-induced activities. This minimum amount is determined by looking at the figures you wrote on your FAFSA.

If a private school costs $70,000 and the Department of Education says your expected family contribution is $10,000, your "need" at that school is $60,000.

$70,000 (Cost of Attendance)
- $10,000 (Expected Family Contribution)
= $60,000 (Financial Need)

It's the financial need that determines how much financial aid your family is *eligible* to receive; however, your need of $60,000 doesn't mean you will be offered $60,000. Pick schools that historically give the best financial aid packages. To this end the College Board website is helpful: www.collegeboard.com. You'll discover that some schools can meet 100% or 60% of your financial need. See section, *After The Award Letters.*

When picking schools find out how much of the "need" they meet is free money, which you never have to pay back, and how much need they meet in "Self-Help" money, which includes work-study and loans you must pay back.

By knowing in advance which schools meet most of your need with more free money and less loans, you'll save yourself the hassle of applying to schools that will never give you enough money. And ask about "front loading": does the school give you more grants in the first year and convert you to more loans later while giving you the same amount of aid? For example, Stafford loans increase automatically each year. Don't ask if they front-load, just assume it by asking, "When do you start converting grants to loans after the freshman year?" If you don't get a fast, positive answer with confidence and certainty from the financial aid counselor, move on to your next choice college.

Planning should be done well before your student's senior year to avoid applying to colleges that will lead you gently and unceremoniously toward personal poverty.

To find this type of information don't bother asking people in the financial aid office. They operate on a policy: "Don't Ask, Don't Tell." If you don't ask the right questions, they don't tell you what you really need to know. Few will volunteer any information, but they'll suggest you visit their college's website. To get more of the info you need, check the College Board website instead, as well as collegeprowler.com, crapcampus.com, and collegedata.com.

Scholarship Highjacking
Colleges Steal Them

A scholarship is free money, right? Well, yes and no. Let's look at two types:

1. College scholarships are awarded directly from the colleges themselves. You don't get a check. Instead you receive a discount on your bill (the bill is the so-called "award" letter, which illustrates how clever with words colleges can be).

2. Private scholarships come from a local group or national organization, and they're not tax-free. Here's the IRS law: *Any amount of the scholarship that is used for room, board, and personal expenses is taxable to the student as income.* Your student absolutely must keep accurate records on the money spent on tuition, college fees, school supplies, and books - everything that is connected directly to being educated. These expenses *are* tax-free. To use the money to swallow gallons of beer every weekend doesn't count. As far as expecting a student to keep records, your expectations for winning the lottery are more realistic.

These scholarships are considered assets by the colleges, and as a result, you are usually penalized at the full confiscatory rate of 100%. For example, if your scholarship is for $1,000, the colleges will subtract this amount of aid from your original award package. It's like being taxed at 100% (read: robbed). Who knew that a private scholarship would become a cash-cow for the colleges? Those colleges who want you bad enough may substitute a pre-determined loan and use your $1,000 instead. I favor this substitute approach, but not all colleges do it. In effect, the college, not you, was awarded the scholarship, a cash gift to the college with your name all over it.

To illustrate, here's one university's stated policy on your private scholarship: "**How are private scholarships incorporated into financial aid awards?**... University need-based aid will not be adjusted when private scholarships are received unless total aid would exceed calculated need." Or, if your scholarship amount makes our original aid package more than what you need by a maximum of $300, we'll adjust the value of your aid package.

"Please inform us," states a typical college award letter, "of any scholarships or funds you expect to receive from outside sources." Never tell a college what you expect; tell only what you have. You may have won a scholarship, or been promised one, but if you don't have the check in your bank, it doesn't exist. According to a federal regulation, colleges require you to inform them of your scholarship so that Uncle Sam isn't getting gouged by the college on its disbursement of federal aid, and if you don't, they will call it fraud. Fair enough. But the *private* colleges dispense federal funds *before* they dispense their own, much of which is raised by overly inflated tuition prices that are gouged automatically each year from parents. Their benign identity as the modern versions of Robin Hood is appropriate: he was no fraudulent character, Hood was just a kind-hearted and well-meaning mugger.

What you have is a contemptible redistribution of wealth by *private* colleges. Most of them are bold enough to tell you right up front that they're handling your scholarship in this manner. Plus, knowing that you're bragging to all your friends about the big scholarship you received from the local Rotary Club, they're counting on your ego to blind you from seeing what they're doing. They understand human nature. You won't know that your private scholarship was literally highjacked by the college. And the Rotary Club won't know that it was the college's unintended accomplice in this legal but shameful theft.

Here's one response to a school that requires the CSS Profile: have the check made out to the parent. If there's any hesitation, show this chapter to the giver and sport a big smile for the local media cameras. Go ahead and accuse me of deception.

21 Income Strategies

Get Money Aid + Save Money

Reducing your Adjusted Gross Income (AGI), which is defined as gross income minus adjustments to income, is a viable strategy and by doing so you'll max your ability to get more aid. Each dollar of income is assessed against you anywhere from 5 to 9 times more than a dollar of assets. Plus, most aid will be determined more by *what you earn than by what you own*.

1. The Two-Income Family The lower wage earner can deduct up to 35% of salary up to the first $8,571 (Most private schools will allow your maximum to be $9,025). It's earned as an "employment allowance." This allows you to reduce your EFC (Expected Family Contribution), which determines what the colleges expect you to pay.

2. Reduce Gross Income If possible ask your employer to separate your business expenses from your income. This too will reduce your AGI and EFC. Check with your accountant on the viability of this strategy.

3. If you own few assets, or possess millions in assets but have an AGI (adjusted gross income) under $50,000 a year, and you can file a 1040A or 1040EZ, your assets are excluded from the federal aid formulas and are not counted against you. You and the millionaire next door will qualify for lots of FREE money. You will pay slightly higher taxes, but you may gain a lot more financial aid. You will pay a little more tax, but you could gain a lot more financial aid.

4. Alternative Minimum Tax It qualifies as a deduction against income just like income taxes. It lowers your EFC.

5. Student Income The student will lose in financial aid 50 cents on every dollar earned over $6,200. Despite its anti-work ethic, consider having your child quit work after earning $6,000. If you don't qualify for need-based aid, encourage your student to make as much money as possible = less money out of your pocket. See section, *College Work Study*.

6. Private College Trick Most private schools which require the CSS Profile (read: private colleges's anal exam of your finances) will assume an incoming freshman made as much as $2,200 during the summer. When the award letter comes, a certain income amount will either be hidden in your EFC number, or fully stated. This pops up on a bill and can be dropped if you protest it, that is, write a matter-of-fact, non-complaining, appeal letter to indicate this expectation, or the actual dollar amount was never indicated on the school's website, thereby hinting at a bait-and-switch tactic by the school without actually saying it. Even if they do list the amount, ask them to justify how they arrived at their cheesy figure. Brace yourself: they won't be able to explain how. Always be positive when communicating with the financial aid office, even when your suspicions are dead-on.

7. Transfer Credit Card Debt and/or Auto Loans Refinancing or taking out a home equity loan to pay off the credit cards and autos will give you a double benefit: (1) deductibility of interest, and (2) lowering your EFC with most *private* schools. Caution: Taking out a *line of credit* does nothing to reduce your EFC; it's reduced only by the amount used, not by the amount approved.

8. Student Loans Try to pay off as much of a loan of a student who has already graduated, or as much as you can while a student is still in college. This will lower your Adjusted Gross Income. Check with your accountant (1040, line 33, Student loan interest deduction).

9. EE Bonds If purchased after 1989, cash them in. These funds will not be part of your EFC if you indicate that the money is being spent on college tuition; the interest paid at redemption time will be tax-free. But if your income is above $119,750, forget it because the income from these bonds will be considered income by the colleges. Solution? Cash them before January 1 of the junior year of high school, or roll them into Series H or HH bonds, report interest only when college is completed, and cash them in to help pay off student loan debt. And the bonds must be titled in the parents' name.

10. Stock Losses Take your losses in mutual funds, stocks, bonds or other investments during the college years up to a max of $3,000/yr (1040 Line 13, Capital gain). Plus, any net losses over $3,000 are carried over to future years. Note: many private schools will recognize losses that exceed gains.

11. Start-up Business Starting your own business during the college years means a lot of start-up costs and sweet business deductions. That means a lower AGI = lower EFC = more financial aid possibilities. Plus, if you have fewer than 100 employees, the net value of your business does not have to be reported on the FAFSA (but will be required information by most private schools). Cash that is in your business account may be considered an asset, but check with an accountant to be sure.

12. Family Business The business pays, say $10,000, to a part-time or low-salaried family member or relative over 18 who doesn't live with you. The $10,000 is subtracted from your AGI which will result in a lower EFC and less taxes. Or, you're in the 28% tax bracket (you likely won't qualify for need-based aid) with a 15-year-old who loves computers. Hire him for $10,000 to do your company's computer work. Your tax savings = $2,500. The child would only have a $500 tax liability [$10,000 - $5,000 (zero tax bracket) x 10%] which is a $2,000 net tax savings. The savings over a 3-year period = $6,000; over 6 years = $12,000. Instead of paying the college with after-tax dollars, it's far better to hire the child and use the earnings to fund a college account that's in your name, not in the student's. A business with less than 100 employees is not an asset that has to be reported on your FAFSA form. *Be absolutely sure to factor into this discussion Item #5 above*, **Student Income**.

13. State + Local Tax Refunds If you collected a refund of, say, $1,600 each year over a 4-year period, you may have lost as much as $3,000 in grants. Consider rolling this money into a 401K. Knowing that you can borrow up to $50,000 or 50%, whichever is the smaller amount, the amount does now show up in your AGI because it's designated as a loan.

14. Tax Credits Most parents qualify for them. They are the American Opportunity Tax Credit (up to $2,500) and The Lifetime Learning Credit (up to $2,000). You could lose some financial aid in these cases, but the gain will surely offset any loss. For each year your child is in college, get IRS Form 8863.

15. Medical Expenses Contact lenses, braces, cab to the doctor's office, or an on-going medical condition - all fit into those medical expenses that are considered in the federal aid formulas. Keep excellent records of out-of-pocket costs. Wave your health insurance premiums like a red flag in front of a financial aid director – it's a legitimate factor as to how much more aid you can receive.

16. ROTH IRAs Consider placing a student's income in a ROTH IRA. Retirement accounts don't count in your EFC, and no penalties or taxes have to be paid on withdrawals for educational expenses after

5 years as long as you're 59 1/2 years of age. Or, if your children are enthusiastically uncommitted to work, pay them up to the maximum of $2,500 each so you can deduct the amount from your AGI. Make certain the $2,500 ends up in your account. Sitting in your child's account means the amount is penalized by at least 20% *each year* the amount remains in the student's name.

17. Alimony/Divorce If your ex is behind in payments, it could mean a lower EFC and more financial aid. Or, in a divorce settlement, the custodial parent should consider getting less income and more assets. Why? The child is likely to receive more financial aid. Side benefit = child gets to witness 2 mature adults place the focus where it belongs - on the child's needs, not on the parents' competing concerns. In short, everybody wins.

18. Selling Your Home Gains above $500,000 per couple are considered income by the colleges, and if you haven't purchased another house, the money sitting in the bank is counted as an asset. A double whammy. Solution? Don't sell your valuable house during the college years. Not selling the house will keep your EFC from going up. Selling your house could mean an increase in EFC.

19. Rollovers When colleges ask for a copy of your tax return, be sure to call attention to any pension or IRA rollover. You will list the rollover on line 15a or 16a of your 1040 tax return, but many colleges make the mistake of assuming that you actually received the funds. Notifying the colleges prevents them from decreasing your financial aid. WARNING: The 1099 reporting form is often miscoded.

20. Recently Unemployed or Disabled Colleges are likely to help you with more aid if you're out of work. They'll likely want proof, such as a termination notice or doctor's statement. You should contact them immediately. Ask the school to exercise what is known as "Professional Judgment." It'll signal that you know how to play the college game, and they'll likely respond in your favor.

21. Retirement Contributions What's already in your retirement account doesn't count against you, but the money you contribute during the college years does. Consider deferring any contributions to your retirement if you think you'll need the money to pay for a high EFC. Don't consider this option until after reading the next chapter.

Asset Strategies

Reposition Your Assets To Get More Aid

Student Savings Account Hit your teenager with the first reality of college: transferring their money into your account as a documented loan. Why? Because most colleges reduce financial aid by 20% per year depending on how much the student has in the bank. For example, if your child has $2,000 in savings, a college will multiply $2,000 X 20% to equal the amount of aid your student will *not* receive. If you keep an on-going balance of $2,000 in the child's account for 4 years, it gets penalized @ $400 each year. That means you'll lose $1,600 in aid over 4 years, thereby making you an involuntary accessory to a robbery of $1,600 by the college.

Roth IRA If you don't want to place a child's income in your account, put it into a ROTH IRA. A child's earned income, not savings, can be placed inside a ROTH. They can withdraw all the money tax-free after 5 years when they've reached 59 1⁄2 years of age. All retirement plan balances are excluded from federal financial aid penalties. Warning: Some private colleges will consider a ROTH a student asset. Call the financial aid office of each college to which your child is applying and ask about their policy on Roths; each college's policy can differ from the other. See Item #17 in the previous chapter.

Asset Protection Allowance As a parent you can keep an amount of cash that isn't counted against you. The Dept of Education allows you money for emergencies based on the age of the older parent. For example, if you're 46 years old, $43,000 is exempt from penalty by the colleges; if you're 54, it's $53,100. If you married an old geezer, you have the benefit of a golden oldie. **Caution:** What the Dept of Ed gives, private colleges can take away. We've seen these colleges treat this "safe" money as a resource by awarding less aid. **Lesson:** When any college is asking for a copy of your tax returns, they're trolling for ways to give you less aid, not just to recheck the numbers on your forms. Whatever is your maximum allowance, be sure you have 20%-30% less in evidence. Where to put the rest? Read the last paragraph of this section.

529s, UGMA/UTMA Accounts & Pre-Paid Plans The slash-your-wrists negatives far outweigh the sales-pitch positives: even though these plans are assessed at 5.6% as a parent asset, you can be penalized at a gargantuan 100%. See section, **529s, UGMAs & UTMAs.**

Legally transfer "includable" assets into "non-includable" assets. Includable assets are penalized by the financial aid formulas. They include cash, savings, checking accounts, mutual funds, real estate, savings bonds, money-market funds, CDs, stocks, and treasury bills. Most private schools include home equity, a farm, and all the assets from the previous paragraph.

Home Equity Don't touch your home equity if your kid's going to a state school. Such schools do not ask about your home equity, but most private schools get excited over the prospect that you have a ton of equity in your home and a secondary residence. Home equity to a private school is a gold mine: they figure you have the gold so they can mine it to their benefit. Colleges don't care that you can cash out a lot of your equity - retirement money? - to help pay for college. That means they won't have to give you a lot of financial aid. They're playing to win, and a lot of equity in your home helps them win big, very big. For every $100,000 you have in equity means you could lose as much as $5,640 in financial aid *each year per child* in college. Gargantuan OUCH!

Modified Endowment Contract (MEC) What if you could take the equity out of your home so that it doesn't count against you? You can reposition it inside a MEC where it's not counted against you. Funds can be accessed largely on a tax-free basis without it being counted as income. Access can begin by taking loans after one year (there's always a waiting period before early withdrawal penalties set in) as partial withdrawals. Another way to justify refinancing is to answer this question: How much money can I *comfortably* put aside each month for education? Take that amount, add it to your current mortgage payment, and refinance now with the cash-out going into a MEC you can use to pay for education or retirement. Before looking at loans, a refi interest rate of, say, 3.2% beats a Parent PLUS loan fixed-rate of 6.4%. After 2 - 3 years the *interest rate you earn on your MEC could exceed 5%,* thereby reducing your true refi rate to less than what you're actually paying. Great lesson here: it's cheaper to borrow from yourself. **Caution:** MECs can be *very complicated*, and as a financial aid strategy, I don't recommend them. Be weary of so-called "college advisors" who strongly recommend them.

Gifting If you don't want to refinance, take out the maximum amount of equity and parcel it out in the tax-free maximum amount of $14,000, as a gift to someone you trust *outside of the immediate family*. In a 2-parent home, both parents can gift a total of $28,000 to the same person. This gifting will devalue your home to a private college, which in turn will qualify you for more financial aid. Once you've settled on a school, and you've received the maximum amount of aid due to taking out the equity and exhausting the appeal process, have your trustworthy friends or relatives legally gift the money back to you. If you gifted $100,000, you'd qualify for $5,000 in financial aid *per child*. Of course, you'll pay interest on the loan you took out, but it'll be more than offset by the aid you receive for, say, 2 children in college at the same time; for one child's benefit, gifting is less attractive because what you gain in aid and what you pay in interest may turn out to be a wash.

Repeat this process each year your children are in college. This approach works very well with close-knit families where trust is a sacred bond. In the example above, 2 children in college could get you an additional $11,200 in financial aid in one year. Are you salivating yet? **Caution:** if the person you gift to is sued for any reason, and a sharp lawyer discovers the house as an asset, gifting will turn into a nightmare.

The strategy of gifting doesn't have to be limited to reducing home equity. You can gift whatever money you have in bank accounts, stocks, bonds, CDs, or mutual funds. The objective is to have all the appearances of being asset poor, destitute, or broke. It's all perfectly legal in a game that's designed to beat you, a game you can win.

Fixed Indexed Annuities (FIA) This is a non-includable asset sold by insurance companies. It has the features of a savings plan: minimum guaranteed interest with no risk of losing either principle or prior gains due to market performance. In other words, whatever money you put into them is subject to the upward moves of the market, never the down ones. It's anti-gravitational: it never goes down in value as it participates only in the market's gains. If the market goes up and you gain 7% or 8% over a 12-month period, say, $700 on $10,000 invested, your new $10,700 stays right where it is if the market takes a dive in the following year. Once it starts to go back up and the market's made a gain for the next year, your $10,700 also goes up in value. Bottom line: *you can't lose any money in a bad year, but you can earn money in a good year*. Or, there's only upside potential with no downside risk. To avoid risking all of your invested money, I encourage my clients to put at least some of their portfolio assets into an FIA. Any monies earned are subject to the 59.5 age rule: there's a 10% penalty for early withdrawal and an ordinary income tax at your tax rate.

Some "elite" colleges will ask if a parent has an annuity or whole life insurance. Tell them it's none of their business because that money is part of your retirement. There's a chance that a college will back off from your defensive posture because they actually expect you to spill your guts and crawl a mile on broken glass to get your child into their sacred institution. Be sure to wear your emotional armor when you make this statement, that is, your attitude should be, "I don't need your school when I have over 4,000 colleges to choose from." Be prepared for the school to hold its ground. This suggestion doesn't work all the time, but it's *delicious* when it does.

To further reduce the cost of college, there are 2 financial vehicles I recommend for repositioned assets: universal life insurance if you need access to the money to pay for college, and FIAs if you don't need immediate access. CAUTION: These vehicles are best taken out years before college comes along, which probably means it's too late for you to consider them now; you would not be reading this book if your college-bound child is 5 years-old. There are plenty of insurance companies which can give you these vehicles with the benefits I described, and financial planners, accountants or insurance agents can guide you in their purchase. See section, *If Your Aid Isn't Enough.*

"...higher education is Teflon-coated, remarkably immune to criticism."

Gene Maeroff
Teachers College
Columbia University

529s, UTMAs & UGMAs

Avoid Them

Don't put a penny into any 529 plans if your child is already in high school. This chapter is directed toward the reader who should have considered this vehicle long before high school was an expectation, let alone college. So herein are the realities to deal with if your child is already a teenager.

Uncle Sam doesn't tax you to use 529 money, but the colleges will. "Sound complicated? It is." So says the head honcho of a 529 marketing website. "And we are only talking about the federal financial aid rules here -- each school can (and most will) set its own rules when handing out its own need-based scholarships, and many schools are starting to adjust awards when they discover 529 accounts in the family." Holy Confusion, Batman! For some clarity, there are 2 types of 529s: a pre-paid plan and a savings plan.

529 Pre-Paid Let's say your 529 has $30,000. Colleges will penalize you dollar-for-dollar. That means you will lose $30,000 in financial aid because, from the perspective of the colleges, you already paid $30,000 for education because that's what "pre-paid" means. Imagine the excitement of financial aid people upon discovery of your pre-paid 529....

529 Savings Plan Colleges penalize you at 5.6% on available assets in the amount of aid you will not receive; for example, if $30,000 were sitting in a savings account, and you chose to spend your money in 4 equal amounts over 4 years, they'll hit you immediately with a penalty of $1,680 in aid you'll never see. With gleeful resolve, colleges will exercise a creative financing genius that makes accountants marvel. They'll continue to penalize you for these funds until you're bled dry. Here's how:

1st year of college: $30,000 X 5.6% = $1,680 lost in financial aid

2nd year of college: $22,500 = 3/4 of 30K X 5.6% = $1,260 lost

3rd year of college: $15,000 = 1/2 of 30K X 5.6% = $840 lost

4th year of college: $7,500 = 1/4 of 30K X 5.6% = $420 lost

Total lost in financial aid = $4,200

In effect, you're penalized, not at 5.6%, but at 14 percent ($4,200 = 14% of $30,000) of the original amount. By getting rid of this 529 as soon as possible to place somewhere else, let's assume two realities: you're in the 28% tax bracket (you earn between $123,700 and $188,450), and your plan earned a gain of $5,000. Here's what hap- pens: you're penalized at 10% on this gain, which is

$500. Plus, your $5,000 is hit with a 28% tax (your 28% tax bracket), which is $1,400. Total loss = $1,900.

Your choices are either to leave your 529 alone at a cost of $4,200 in lost financial aid, or spend every dime in the first year. Or, transfer the 529 into a savings account as long as the amount comes under your Asset Protection Allowance, or move the money into a non-includable asset. Either of these two transfers would cost you $1,900 in taxes and penalty. These moves not only produce a difference of $2,300 in your favor ($4,200 - $1,900 = $2,300), but a non-includable asset can be accessed for any purpose with little or no penalty. Don't you just love a no-brainer?

With the best of intentions, like cash, your 529 savings plan became a scholarship program you created all by yourself for the college's benefit. Visualize the giddiness of everyone in the college's financial aid office upon learning of *your* 529 plan, which you are required to list on line 88 of your FAFSA form.

A pre-paid 529 is a reverse subsidy program. Instead of colleges giving you aid, you're giving them aid. It's in the form of freeing up $30,000 for the colleges to give to someone else. In this example, the $30,000 you would have received, if you did not own a 529 plan, is parceled out to other students who don't have one. That's why my clients are grateful for the aid they receive from parents with pre-paid 529 plans. And because both types of 529s are tax-free at spending time, people easily buy the 529 sales pitch without ever questioning the pitcher.

A 529 in a younger sibling's name will also be counted against the entering student at most *private* schools. More damage. You could have the 529 money be in the name of a grandparent because the FAFSA doesn't ask about grandparent assets; however, a *private* college which requires the CSS Profile will ask you about assets that will come from other family members or *relatives* with line item SR-165B. Last I heard, a grandparent is a relative.

Caution: If you start a small business and designate the *business* as the owner of the 529 plan, it doesn't mean that a college will exempt what's in the plan. The net value of a small business that has less than 100 employees is not counted as an asset on the FAFSA form, but a private college that requires the CSS Profile can still exercise the right to count your 529 as a big, fat, delicious asset.

UGMAs and UTMAs (Uniform Gift and Uniform Transfer to Minors Act Accounts) are trust accounts that have terrific punishment-promise because they're considered a student asset. You're hit with a penalty of at least 20 percent (up to 30% at private colleges). That means, using our $30,000 example, you stand to lose a minimum of $6,000 in financial aid in the *first* college year. If you spent this money in equal amounts over 4 years, your effective penalty is not 20%, but a whopping 50%, or $15,000 in lost aid. That's a generous subsidy for another student who doesn't own an UGMA. UTMAs work the same way. Warning: this money is an irrevocable asset of the child. That means they own it, and when they reach legal age (18 or 21), they can spend it any way they want. If you spend it before the legal age, you can be sued later by the child for the entire amount. Have you hugged your child today?

Other Pre-Paid Tuition Plans: You're mugged for 100%, dollar-for-dollar. In our $30,000 example, you would lose $30,000 in financial aid because you have this plan. Okay...it still beats having bought swamp land in Florida.

For information on how to legally reposition the money in these programs, to get off the college's radar screen of penalties and assessments, and qualify for more aid, see section, *Asset Strategies.*.

Reality Check #1 Since 529 money is invested with after-tax dollars in a range of investment options, usually mutual funds, what do you suppose will happen to the value of your 529 on the very day there's another stock market crash or another version of 9/11? With more predictable terrorist attacks in the United States, or something as foreign as the Zika virus - fears that drive market volatility - your 529 will likely tank or blow up, and then it'll take years for the value to get back to where it was before these catastrophes. *Is this any way to protect money that's designated for college?*

Reality Check #2 If a 529 plan is purchased in the early years of the student's life, there are attractive tax benefits for the family and/or grandparents. A financial planner, with education planning as part of his or her services, is a valuable source for more details of the 529 advantages.

Start A Business Now
More Financial Aid + Tax Advantages

Affording college includes saving on what you pay in taxes. A business has tax right-offs because of expenses. If you've always wanted to have your own business, you can start small with something right out of your house. The internet is chock-full of ideas of what you can do right now. For financial aid purposes, you shouldn't care if you don't want to own a business. There's a huge advantage without the headaches, which I'll mention shortly. What follows is what you can save when you hire your children to work in your business. It's a 3-step process:

(1) Establish an unincorporated business, and hire your under-18 year-olds who must be over 6 years of age. Pay them "reasonable wages" (not $50K for filing, but $5K for computer work which makes sense to the IRS) even if your business doesn't show a profit. There are no federal withholding income taxes. Work can be full or part-time.

(2) Prove the Deduction Keeping excellent records is a must. Keep a time-sheet and pay your child with a check. The check can be endorsed over to you for deposit into your account to pay for college expenses. It's better that the child's savings be in your account before Dec 31 of the junior year so that it's penalized less by the colleges before submitting those complicated financial aid forms.

(3) Give each child a W-2 at the end of the year. And file a tax return. Let's look at an example. You have 2 teenagers under 18. Pay each one up to the maximum standard deduction of $6,300 (in 2016), which means the first $6,300 of income is not taxed. Any extra money earned is taxed at 10%. Check with your accountant first to see how well this works.

Net Result: You paid your children $12,600 ($6,300 X 2) that you can deduct, and it's tax-free to them. If you're in the 20% tax bracket, you saved yourself $2,520 in federal taxes alone; if you're in the 25% bracket, you saved $3,150 in a year.

There can be additional savings. If possible, pay each child an additional $4,000 to be sheltered in a ROTH IRA, keeping in mind that there's a $400 tax. The total savings on each child would now be $8,350 ($4,750 + $4,000 - $400 tax), or $16,700 tax-free. Each child was paid $8,350 tax-free, and the parent gets a deduction of

$16,700 with a tax savings of $3,340 (20% tax bracket), or $4,175 (25% tax bracket).

Caution #1: If you've done everything right, there should be no problem. The only issue the IRS could raise is the "reasonableness" of what you paid your child. Work can be any combination of computer work, sweeping floors, filing documents, washing windows, stocking inventory, or making deliveries. The work needs to be evident and preferably on-going. And if the business takes a loss because it's a start-up, you could receive more financial aid because your earnings will be less.

Caution #2: In the above example, the $8,350 earned in the student's senior year will be assessed against the student at 50% above the first $6,200. That's $8,350 minus $6,200 = $2,150 X 50% = $1,075. That's $1,075 which a college will NOT give your child in financial aid that year. The loss isn't cool, but you've got more money put away, and your child's development of a solid work ethic is a big positive for everybody.

Here's the large advantage to owning a business while your children are in college: the net value of a family-owned business with less than 100 employees does not have to be reported as an asset on the FAFSA form. Sweet! You can make owning a business part of your winning strategy in the college game. Caution: this won't work with private schools that require the CSS Profile.

Best Kept Secret
Community Colleges

If you're broke, or your child is an under-achiever or totally without radar on his future, or the cost of a 4-year college is simply prohibitive, take a serious look at a community college. Grades and SATs don't matter. All you need for admission is a heartbeat and a checkbook. The costs are much less than either public or private 4-year schools. They account for 1,100 of the more than 4,000 schools in America today. As costs continue to skyrocket, community colleges will become more popular. And rightfully so.

The makeup of community colleges closely resembles the small class sizes, the high degree of personal interaction between students, between students and faculty, and a genuine student motivation that are found at small elite liberal arts colleges. These similarities are a parent's dream. As for parents who are distressed about their student's motivation, Dr Thomas E. Gamble, president of Florida's Brevard Community College, says "the community college deals effectively with the student malaise of under-achievers."

A student gave this real-life assessment of the community college experience: "The diversity of the student body, the number of people taking part-time courses, and the lack of residence halls and meal plans (at least at my CC) taught me a lot about self-reliance, money and time management, and removed me from an environment of parties and drinking that would have potentially led me down a path to bad grades and low achievement." This is what every parent would love to read of their student who's attending a 4-year college.

Admissions directors of high-profile 4-year colleges hold a near universal opinion of these 2-year schools. "Community colleges," says an admissions dean at a Connecticut university, "do a fine job of preparing students to go on to higher education." Instead of being a last resort to higher education, they're effective gateways to higher-level degrees.

From an admissions standpoint, it's easier to be accepted to a 4-year college as a community college transfer than as a high school senior; 33% of applicants to UC Berkeley were accepted from community colleges compared to 28% from high school applicants. Miami Dade College, a community college in Florida with a separate honors program for high-achieving students who aren't ready for the usual 4-year college experience, has agreements with over 50 universities. Nearly half go on to colleges like the University of Wisconsin, Georgia Tech, Cornell, Smith, Yale, and the University of Texas.

The first 2 years of a college education can cost a parent nothing. Here's how it works: the student commutes to a local community college with tuition and books for about $4,500. Add from $500 to $1,000 in transportation expenses, and the total approximates $5,500 a year. The student takes out a Stafford Loan in the first year for $5,500, which the student pays back, not the parent. Plus, a summer job for 15 weeks, with a weekly take-home pay of only $150 generates $2,250. So, $5,500 minus the Stafford's $5,500 + the student's $2,250 = still $0 out of the parent's pocket.

In the second year, the student qualifies for more money with a Stafford Loan: $6,500. It's another year free of costs for mom and dad. Talk about liberation! Whoa! Yes! You're free of the high costs of college which your friends will pay because they didn't follow the advice you're reading now.

With a game plan to get a degree from a 4-year college, the first 2 years are free to the parents, and the student can qualify for Stafford loans as a transfer student in the junior and senior years of a state school for $7,500 each year. That's another $15,000 parents don't have to pay toward a 4-year degree. In other words, your child can get a 4-year degree from an in-state state school at half the price of other schools, or less. Could this be planet earth's easiest no-brainer? It gets better.

Here's the math for a parent's out-of-pocket costs:

· 1st yr of community college: $0 (Stafford pays $5,500 and the student's earnings make up for the smaller balance, if any)

· 2nd yr of community college: $0 (Stafford pays $6,500 and the student's earnings make up for a smaller balance, if any)

· 3rd yr of 4-year state school in the Northeast (most expensive schools): $17,000 (includes room & board) minus a Stafford Loan of $7,500 = $9,500 out-of-pocket; the parent pays little or nothing if the student is commuting.

· 4th yr of 4-year state school in the Northeast: see year 3.

Stafford loans in the 1st year amount to $5,500, and in the 2nd year, $6,500. With a very little income-paying job, your student can easily pay the first 2 years of college. Fast-forward to your total out-of-pocket expenditure for a 4-year state school degree as a campus resident: from $10,000 to $21,000. If your student is *commuting in the 3rd and 4th years*, the range in costs could be from $5,000 to $10,000. But here's the mind-blowing secret that allows a parent to pay nothing in the last 2 years:

You can pay absolutely nothing for your student's 4-year degree. This is the best kept secret about paying for college, revealed for the first time - right here. Now you don't have to read Ben Kaplan's *How To Go To College Almost For Free,* because he says, *"Almost."*

This secret comes with 2 bonuses: (1) in 2 years, you can graduate with an Associates degree with at least a 2.5 GPA and you're *automatically* admitted to an in-state 4-year state school as a junior. States such as Florida, Massachusetts and Wisconsin offer such a program; and (2) proudly you can claim you worked your way through college, made the daily sacrifices that struggling parents make, and demonstrated a maturity, a work ethic, and an achievement that no Harvard graduates can put on their resumes.

You win. And win big.

What's the downside for the student? S/he has to live at home for 4 years. The upside? S/he gets to BOND with mommy and daddy for another 4 years!

"I have found that a demanding professor who might be a good teacher but refuses to do the 'dog and pony show' for the students, and grades without inflation, will tend to get low evaluations [from students]. However, the professor who attempts to be personable with the students while asking little academically, and inflates grades, will get high evaluations. Sounds a little like the prisoners are running the prison, doesn't it?"

R. Terry Ervin
Eastern New Mexico University

College Award Letters
The Award = The Bill

What you have to pay for college, which is found in the so-called "award letter," reads like a utility bill. Typical is one that offered a student a bank of emotional steroids, designed to pump up his enthusiasm for the school - a grant for $6,000 for the first year. Free bucks. No pay-back. What followed next was a titanic offer to sink the family's finances: over $28,000 in loans in the first year. It was the family's Commencement Exercise in the economic realities of the college money game.

Look for the amount that none of the grants and loans will cover. You'll be forced to do the math. Take the cost of attendance, less the aid package = your out-of-pocket costs.

Note the conditions to keep what's offered. Is the offer good for 4 years? Or, if your student is one of near 70% of the incoming freshman class this year who will graduate in 5 years, will the aid package be good for all 5 years? Sorry...that's a dumb question.

Does the school indicate that a private scholarship is deducted? Some colleges will substitute your scholarship for a loan to lessen your loan liability, but other colleges see scholarships as a gift to themselves. See section, **Scholarship Highjacking.**

"Award" is a superbly seductive word that is similar to the word "fee," which local governments use in order to hide the word "tax." Colleges use words like "award" as part of their cheerleading vocabulary to pillage your savings.

Never underestimate a college's trademark ability to exercise creative financing at your expense. You may not even notice it with the feel-good language they use, but it'll be right there in the "award" letter, so obvious you're likely to miss it.

Some *private* colleges are clever in how they decrease their aid packages. One Ivy League school sent one of my students an award notification saying that his "Summer Savings Expectation" was $2,180 - aid the college wouldn't give because they expected the student to earn it during the summer prior to the fall semester. The standard formula of penalizing the student for his assets (20%) or for his earnings (50% of every dime earned over $6,200) was ignored by the college. Instead the school penalized the student at 100% of any amount earned *under* $2,180 – this from a college with an endowment of $4,300,000,000 (Did you count all those zeros?). America's oldest Catholic college in Washington DC was less punishing: $1,700 as a "Student Contribution from Income." This college told my client that expected expenses for the 2015-2016 academic year would be $62,570. Breath-taking, isn't it?

Such obscenities are also generated by so-called prestigious academic institutions. To deal with them, see section, **22 Income Strategies**, **#6**.

Award Letter Mistakes, or Pure Smoke An award letter can have a missing Stafford loan, work study, or Pell Grant for which the student automatically qualifies. Or, the Ivy League school mentioned above meets 100% of a family's need, but used this truly astonishing smoke screen to discourage a father from appealing his son's aid package: "The emergency reserve allowance and cumulative education savings allowance protect the assets. The emergency reserve allowance (ERA) that we are using is $27,180. The cumulative education savings allowance (CESA) we are using is $64,279. Once these allowances are made against your total available assets of $316,913, we use a formula looking at 5%, not 5.6%. The calculation would then be $316,913 (total assets) minus $91,459 (asset allowances) which equals your discretionary net worth. As you have assets over $59,200 we use the formula $225,444 minus $59,200 multiplied by 5% plus $2,070. This gives us a total asset contribution of $10,383."

Get it? Neither did I.

"Harvard students...often graduate without the core knowledge one would or should expect. One of [Harvard president] Summers's remedies was to have faculty teach more, especially more overview courses that afford students an introduction to different disciplines. The faculty was resistant....As a tenured professor responded when asked to teach an introductory art history survey, 'No self-respecting scholar would want to teach such a course.'"

Mortimer B. Zuckerman, Editor-in-Chief,
US News & World Report, 4/10/2006

After The Award Letters
Get More Money

Most parents, on the seemingly credible but expensive advice of their plumber or hairdresser, regard the award letter as a document cast in stone. It's not an award letter, it's a paper sedative to lessen the jolt you're receiving by what is truly the bill. Hopefully you've received more than one award letter, so don't lock on to the letter that offers the most aid, but the letter that has you paying the least out-of-pocket. It's not what you get in financial aid, it's what you keep for your retirement. After all, college is a retirement issue. And retirement comes before college expenses because you can always get a loan for college, but you can't get one for retirement.

Either before you apply, or after receiving all the aid you're going to get, call the school's financial aid office and ask them to walk you through your out-of-pocket costs. Discuss the typical campus expenses, like health insurance fees that are never mentioned in a school's catalog. It'll open your eyes and help you decide which school is most affordable. See section, **College Money Traps**.

Every spring the tables turn. "April," said T.S. Eliot, "is the cruelest month," not so much for you, but for the schools. Except for the most selective colleges and universities, the fate of the nation's colleges is now in the hands of 17- and 18-year olds. It's the colleges' turn to be nervous, waiting to see if *they* will be accepted or rejected. It's not unusual for a major university to mail 18,000 acceptance letters to fill 4,000 slots. That means 14,000 picky teenagers will reject the school. It's nail-biting, high-stakes academic poker for the colleges, and your student is holding nearly all the cards. Play them to the max, but how?

Appeal. Pleading with cookies, cakes, and food baskets don't work; it's tacky. In a non-threatening manner, always begin by thanking the college for their aid package. It sets a positive tone that greases your way to win. Simply convey in an email - *never call* - that you have a problem accepting the school's offer because it doesn't meet the amount of aid you were hoping to receive - what you need, which may force you to consider another school. Or, state that the school isn't matching a better offer. Instead of making other schools request that you fax another school's better offer, include it (or include all better offers) with your appeal letter. It will command their attention, which will concentrate their effort to offer you something better. State schools are not likely to help you, but private schools can, which is why you should apply to at least 10 colleges to get as many offers as possible. More offers potentially give you more leverage. Some schools will simply say that they're not influenced by another school's offer. Don't believe it for a second. Write another appeal, and *always* with a positive tone.

If you have a better offer from another college, suggest a discount on tuition, and if you don't mind working, ask where on campus you can get a job. Each year thereafter repeat the request. Over 4 years it could mean thousands of dollars in additional financial aid. This is how you beat the colleges at their own money game.

Colleges minimize the dollar amount in their "awards" because they're gambling that you'll accept whatever they offer. Unfortunately, they win most of the time because most parents don't appeal - it never crosses their minds. To increase the college's offer, simply ask *every year*, especially if you got nowhere in the first year. For each of our clients we use a creative appeal strategy that glove-fits their circumstances. You must see section, **Getting The Most Aid.**

The student, rarely the parent, signs my get-to-the-point appeal letter. Financial aid directors, many of whom are parents themselves, are more motivated to make you feel better with a little more money than to give you a generous aid package. Moreover, send a copy of your appeal to the admissions office. There's no guarantee they will fight for you, but the admissions department accepted you for all their right reasons. What do you stand to lose if you don't ask?

Colleges have an appeal allowance that is never disclosed in college catalogs. It's a college's best public relations hammer to nail down your commitment to help make their April peptic seizures go away. Appeals for more aid are particularly effective with all colleges when there's a recent lay-off of one parent, divorce, or some event that signals an economic hardship in the months ahead. In these cases, documentation will be required, and colleges will use what is known as "Professional Judgment" to make a decision on matters that don't fit their standard formulas. In most cases, families receive more aid. This is a great public relations opportunity for a college, a rare moment where you can witness a college helping you win in the college money game.

Unless a college has agreed to meet 100% of your need for more money, you can use my 3-Strikes-And-You're-Out guideline: appeal your award until you are denied 3 times. If you don't know what to say after the first refusal, send a copy of the original letter with a hand-written sticky note requesting reconsideration. A second and third rejection will require a little more creativity. And always send your appeals by Priority Mail with a Delivery Receipt requested.

> To avoid the ultimate public relations disaster, colleges would never revoke your admission or their original financial aid offer just because your student was a nuisance about asking for more. Message to families: *Ask For More!*

Watch for this clever public relations ploy by the colleges: their phone call. After admitting your student, a college is ready to cozy up. Their phone call is the heart-pounder that declares, "We're family now." And then, "We're awarding your student another two thousand dollars because of your request for help." Do *not* express excitement. Respond with a dull "Thank you, but I'd appreciate confirmation in writing." On the other hand, if you hear the college official deny your request for more aid, you can start stumbling and mumbling. No matter what, give the same exact reply. Their call is your signal to begin writing your next appeal letter. The letter should never ask for more money; however, it should ask for more *help*. It's not what you say, it's how you play it.

Lots of acceptance letters increase your chances for more offers of aid. One of my students applied to 14 colleges. Admittedly he applied to many on a whim. Within 11 days, a whim college responded with $76,000 in grants to be used over 4 years. She was suddenly in the grips of a Rodney Dangerfield moment: a college responding so fast with so much free money must have made a mistake. But quantity gave her quality: I used the grant letter to leverage more money from the school of her choice, an extra $8,000 to be exact.

A very smart student wasn't so lucky. He applied to only one school. Not very smart. After receiving his acceptance letter, there was one problem: he was forced to take the Mister Scrooge Scholarship, the minimum offered by the school. Though the student got what he wanted, his parents got what they didn't want: a heaving case of heartburn, a full bag of regrets, and a retirement account going south.

If Your Aid Isn't Enough
Try These Alternatives

Some schools, particularly the private colleges and universities, which have large endowments (read: big bucks growing in investments seemingly without purpose), have more flexibility when it comes to your appealing a better financial aid package. State colleges have very little room to offer anything. Infamous bank robber, Willie Sutton, would remind you to keep your eyes on private schools - that's where the money is.

Understand all payment options available to you just in case the college your child is dying to go to comes up short when offering you financial aid.

Start At A Community College And Then Transfer.
If your student gets accepted to both private and state schools, and they prefer to go to one of the private schools, the first thing you need to look at is how much it is really going to cost you to send him/her to that school.

If the private university offers you an excellent package, which makes it approximately the same cost to you as the state school, your decision is fairly easy; however, if the private university offers you a less-than-competitive package, and sending your student there will put you both in serious debt, my recommendation is to send your child to a community college for two years and then transfer. See section, *Best Kept Secret.*

If your student wants to transfer to a private university but doesn't plan on working for top grades (B+ or better), transferring won't happen. Also, schools tend not to offer their best aid packages to transfer students.

Send Your Student To A College That Offers Cooperative Education.
About 900 colleges and universities across the country offer programs that students can alternate between full-time study and a full-time job. This differs from work-study in that work-study jobs tend to be part-time jobs until the amount of the award is earned. Downside: it may take 5 years or more to graduate. Yuk.

On the upside, cooperative education offers periods of full-time employment in jobs that the student is interested in pursuing after graduation.

Go Military.
There's ROTC (Reserve Officer Training Corps). To qualify for an ROTC Scholarship, which usually covers full or partial tuition plus an allowance of $100/mo, your student must apply in the senior year of high school. Above-average grades and above-average SAT scores are a must.

Apply to one of the military academies. Your student must have top grades and SAT scores, pass a rigid physical, and have a recommendation from a Congressman or Senator. It's a free education if you can meet the high standards, and it'll require a commitment to military service for several years.

Borrow The Money.
Look at federally subsidized loans, which are interest-free until your child graduates, and you have 10 years to repay. The Parent PLUS loan's fixed interest rate is 6.4%. You can get the same loan through a number of private lenders at a reduced rate. Students with bad-credit parents can qualify for more money under the unsubsidized Stafford Loan. If your college offers you a parent PLUS or Stafford loan, ask if you can go through a private lender for the same loan. If they say, "No," it's because they claim that going through them is more cost-effective. When a college is handling our tax-payer money in the form of these loans, my confidence level is about a quarter-inch deep and my BS meter goes off the charts.

The Signature Student Loan is appealing. Your student gets the loan from Sallie Mae, a parent cosigns it, and you don't have to pay anything until the student graduates. After you make 24 on-time payments of principal and interest, the parent's signature disappears and the student is on the hook for the rest of the loan. But s/he gets to start paying it back with his or her first job. If your student doesn't know what career to pursue, or what college to attend, and it turns out that s/he wants to drop out, or flunks out, you didn't spend any of *your* money in the first year. But if the student remains in school, you can always help pay off the loan on the back end (after graduation), instead of on the front end (before admission). This way you played it safe, protected your money, and if there's a drop-out, you didn't lose any money; if there's a stay-in, you have the choice of helping your student pay off the loan 4 years later. **Caution:** this particular loan, like most private-lender loans that need tighter regulation, can be the most expensive. Some have interest rate caps of 18%, 24%, or no caps. Check carefully the fine print before you decide.

Move heaven and earth to avoid taking pre-59½ taxable distributions from your retirement funds to pay for college. That's because you're penalized three ways: (1) you're taxed on the extra income you have to report; (2) you're taxed on the withdrawal you make; and (3) because you increased your EFC by increasing your income, you qualify for less aid. For every dollar you withdraw from your retirement accounts, it could cost you up to 50 cents on the dollar in lost financial aid.

Consider a home equity loan, or a new cash-out refinance of your mortgage since all of your interest payments, which will likely be less than the government's 8.5%, will be tax-deductible. Home equity loans are very popular. It's always possible that a refinance will be cheaper than taking out a home equity loan. Contact your mortgage broker to find out what percentage rate is working today.

There's a strategy that is virtually unknown to banks, colleges, or financial planners. It's using the equity in your home in conjunction with a MEC to lower your EFC. See section, *Asset Strategies.* **Caution:** some college financial planners take a cookie-cutter approach by suggesting you refinance and put the cash-out into a MEC or an annuity, as if to suggest there's no other way to pay for a college education. Bottom line: MECs can be very complicated.

"As faculties are pressed to do more in various areas it is easier to give good grades than hold students to a higher standard."

George Kuh
Director, Indiana University Center for
Postsecondary Research

Attendance
What Every Student Must Know

That most famous and entertaining of American philosophers, Woody Allen, once declared that 80% of life is just showing up. Attending class is no tough requirement. But college students at many colleges get extra credit for attending every class. It's like getting paid extra money for showing up to work everyday. Message to students: learning isn't a priority, but appearances are. Message to parents: higher education is getting lower.

Allen would no doubt agree with this student from the University of North Dakota: "Attend class all the time. You may not think that going to class has anything to do with financial aid, but if you get put on probation, there is a chance that you could have your financial aid revoked. Financial aid is a wonderful thing, don't take it for granted."

_____

"Although we [professors] all give lip service to classroom instruction, there's simply no reward in it. Teaching doesn't advance your career. In fact, it holds you back. As Penn State University scholar James Fairweather has shown, professors who spend more time on instruction-related activities make lower salaries. The more time you devote to research, meanwhile, the more money you earn. These numbers hold constant across different types of institutions, from so-called 'Research-One' universities to liberal arts colleges."

Jonathan Zimmerman
professor, New York University

US News & World Report
College Issue: The Ranking Of Colleges

Except for population figures, addresses, phone numbers, and cost estimates, it's useless.

Note: This page is arguably the shortest chapter in the history of American non-fiction.

College Work-Study
A Great Opportunity?

What is it? Your student can work on or off campus for 10-12 hours a week in the library, book store, cafeteria, study hall, or labs. It's minimum wage and no heavy lifting. It can be as high as $4,500 a year, split equally between 2 semesters.

2 Benefits (1) Your resume for post-college employment will demonstrate that you did something constructive and valuable with some of your spare time at college, thereby signaling a work ethic that'll impress prospective employers, and (2) you developed a time management skill so you could balance your studies with your work. Since college is *always* resume-building time, evidence of work-study on your resume will be a huge plus after college.

Work Ethic For those colleges which give you a work-study program, it may mean they're impressed with your desire to participate in the cost of your own education. How do you make that impression? Do it after you get your award letter if work-study isn't listed. To request it, put it in writing to read like this: "I would very much appreciate being considered for work-study since I intend to pay for most of my education." How many requests do you think a college receives like this from a *student*? Very few.

If you're applying to a college that requires the CSS Profile, which asks about a sibling's assets, make sure that each of the children's accounts has less than $100. Then the student should tell the financial aid office in writing that the parents are requiring you to help pay for your own education. On the other hand, if you ask for work-study when you have $23,000 in your savings account, or your baby-brother's account has $23,000, you have no credibility. The folks in the financial aid office will treat your request as the Joke of the Day.

Part of getting into the right-fit college and getting what you want is making a first good impression. As the schools are marketing themselves to you, you must be marketing yourself to them. It's how to win the college admission game.

Bad hours There's a real job waiting for you, but your work schedule is conflicting with your class schedule. And there's nothing you can do to change it. So you have to decline the work.

Appeal You can appeal this result because the conflict in scheduling wasn't the fault of the student. Believe it or not, you may get some money because you told the financial aid office, "My family was really counting on that money. I purposely listed work-study because I need to help pay for my own education. What can you do to help me in this predicament?" Where there are mothers working in financial aid offices, pulling at heart-strings can work. But pull gently with determination.

Alternative Strategy When you see work study listed on your award letter, chances are good the work study schedule will *not* conflict with your class schedule. But treat it as a *negative* feature of your total award. Tell the college that you do not have a crystal ball to see if your work study hours will conflict with any last-minute changes in your class schedule, and that you fear your work study will turn out to be a non-award, thereby putting you at greater financial risk. So go for the gold: indicate your gratitude for the work-study if there's no conflict, and just in case, indicate that a discount on your tuition would be appreciated.

Another plus The work-study income is not considered income in the financial aid formulas, which means it will not be counted against the student on next year's FAFSA form.

GARGANTUAN WARNING: Work study is never guaranteed. It's available on a first come, first-served basis. But this fact is never disclosed in the award letter. In other words, *work study is a fraudulent entry in your award letter.* You'd better contact the college for email verification on how their work study really works.

"...the reading proficiency of college graduates has declined in the past decade...Only 31 percent of college graduates can read a complex book and extrapolate from it. That's not saying much for the remainder."

Federal Study,
National Center for Education Statistics,
Comments by Lois Romano,
Washington Post, 12/25/05

The 3 Little Pigs of Financial Aid
Will Your Pig Fly?

When the Taxpayer Relief Act of 1997 was passed, Uncle Sam gave a tax credit for college tuition and fee payments. Faster than you could spell G-R-E-E-D, enterprising colleges raised their tuition rates to match the tax breaks. In effect, colleges robbed you of your tax credit - legally. And amazingly, the FAFSA requires you to list this credit in Worksheet C, question 86, as additional income. These credits come in the form of 3 little pigs, or, what looks like a big tax break is really a tiny, iddy-biddy one.

Pig #1. The American Opportunity Tax Credit: You can receive a tax credit of up to $2,500 per student for tuition and fees not in excess of $2,000 plus 25% of those expenses in excess of $2,000 but not to exceed $4,000. "A tax credit," says the IRS, "reduces the amount of income tax you have to pay. Unlike a deduction, which reduces the amount of income subject to tax, a credit directly reduces the tax itself." This pig has lipstick, which means there's hope for some tax relief, even if it's not the full $1,800.

Pig #2. The Lifetime Learning Credit: You may be able to claim the Lifetime Learning Credit of up to $2,000 for qualified education expenses paid for all students enrolled in eligible post-secondary educational institutions. There is no limit on the number of years the lifetime learning credit can be claimed for each student. **Caution:** It's a credit per tax return, and you can't use it in combination with the Pig #1. To get the benefit of either credit, your adjusted joint incomes cannot exceed $127,000. For higher incomes, try...

Pig #3. The Tuition and Fees Tax Deduction is $4,000 if your adjusted gross income (AGI) on a joint return is not more than $160,000. Whatever lipstick you find here disappears when you realize you can't get the full benefit if you take this deduction, itemize your deductions, or claim more than 3 exemptions. The deduction is claimed "as an adjustment to income" on Form 1040, line 35.

TIP #1: Embrace Pig #1 in the first 2 years of college and the Lifetime Learning Credit for the remaining years.

TIP #2: If you didn't file for any of these credits/deductions in the past, ask your accountant if you can file an amended return

(1040X) for the applicable year(s) to get money back from the IRS. Chances are good that a little stash of cash is waiting for you.

TIP #3: Ask colleges if they count your tax credit as income. If they do, ask that they drop this penalty. Why? Because the credit was established in the Taxpayer Relief Act to give financial *relief* to parents. But many colleges count this legal credit as added income. It's an immoral excuse to give you less aid. In sum, a college is penalizing you for taking a legitimate, Congressionally-approved, family-helping, deficit-reducing and a financially stress-relieving credit. Colleges violate the most basic moral principle of justice. Tell the college that you're simply asking for fairness. The result may be a pleasant surprise since colleges rarely see this complaint. It's called "push-back" and you should do it when the opportunity arises.

Put the colleges on notice that you're not the typical unquestioning parent. Never give a college the slightest control over your money, and at all times, when communicating, be pleasant, but business-like in your tone.

Your accountant may be intimately familiar with these 3 little pigs. If you qualify for one, at least one pig will fly.

"Our student financial aid system supports the 'investment in me' approach by making less money available in the form of grants to needy students, and more in the form of loans to be paid back as a return on the individual's investment in themselves. The message our kids get is that they're not students; they're consumers. And if they're willing to settle for 'purchasing' a degree that means nothing in terms of educational achievement, it's their right. It's their investment. In this environment, professors, colleges, and universities are forced into giving the customers what they want, not necessarily what they *should* want."

John Merrow

Drive Colleges Crazy
The Infamous Multiple Deposit

As many as 70% of accepted students won't show up for the fall semester. Colleges want you to send in your deposit by the usual May 1st deadline in order to guarantee your child a place in the freshman class. That's because the good folks in the admissions office expect to suffer from ESPD, Expected Student Population Disorder. They're nervous about not really knowing the exact number of students who will actually attend, or, that 70% of the students they accept will not attend. Even colleges bite their nails at the prospect of getting rejected by a terrific bunch of 17- and 18-year-olds every May. So what's behind the ESPD that drives the college admission departments crazy? Multiple depositing.

Multiple depositing defined: sending deposits to more than one college. Or, what I like to call *weaponizing* your money.

After your student has been accepted at several colleges, but can't make up his or her mind which to attend, hedge your bets. Send your top 2 or 3 colleges their required deposit by May 1st to signal that you're coming (but you're not sure yet). You want to make sure there's a place for your student who's been accepted, but s/he needs more time to decide. The colleges want to assume that your deposit represents a guarantee to attend their school. Because they are aware of this practice of multiple deposits, or kids not making up their minds, they're annoyed by parents who do it.

Why? Because they claim a parent is buying a slot that prevents someone else from getting it. You've denied someone a place at their university by sending in a deposit that signals you've decided to go there. "Unlike the airlines that don't have to guarantee you a seat," said one dean of admissions, "we have to guarantee you a bed when we receive your deposit." And, lo and behold, your student goes elsewhere. The colleges say this result is an unfair body-blow to the student who lost the slot, as if to suggest that the student who lost didn't commit the mortal sin of also making multiple deposits. Talk about spin: what the schools are really saying is that multiple depositing is an unfair body-blow to them. Schools would love life to be fair (read: everything on their terms).

How would you react to this enrollment card that was sent from a "prestigious" Pennsylvania college to one of my students?

Please note: We reserve the right to withdraw the admissions of any student who expresses an intent to enroll in more than one college. (Italics added)

This is similar to a store owner telling you that if you *intend* to shop at more than one competitive store, you may not be allowed to shop in his store. That you *intend* is an over-the-top violation of the Restraint of Trade language in the Sherman Antitrust Act. The store owner would be violating the law. Some "elite" colleges aren't resistant to breaking the law or intimidating an unsuspecting 18-year-old. It never crosses the minds of college officials that they are indeed breaking the law.

Ultimately you shouldn't care what colleges think. This is your student's future and your hard-earned money that are at stake. In reality the college's focus is not on your kid's future or your money, it's on *their* future and *their* money, not to mention the unknown number of students who are going to show up in September. Colleges constitute an industry that, like every other business, dislikes the vagaries and uncertainties of the marketplace. It's antacid time at the admissions office. You've discovered another way to win the college money game.

Sometimes the schools end up with a few empty rooms, and sometimes they're renting motel rooms. Because admissions and financial aid constitute a game that was devised long ago by the colleges who made the rules, are parents required to care if the opponent loses? Are you required to feel guilty when your student wins? Don't hold your breath waiting for a college to cheer your victory.

Colleges have a silver lining in their cloud. Because the college game is all about money, they've already factored in, based on past Septembers, the approximate but inexact number of students who will show up. They forget this is not a marriage transaction, but a business decision that parents must make to their own advantage.

Score to win: weaponize your money by making those multiple deposits.

Wait-Listed
It Could Be Profitable

A website for college admissions people suggested that "...a wait list can be a softer way to reject otherwise well-qualified applicants. But the lists mainly function as insurance for schools to hit their enrollment goals..." With so many applicants these days, so the thinking goes, colleges have the pick of the crop. "I may need to fill liberal arts students," says the admissions director of Duke. "I may want to enroll some from North Carolina, the West Coast or overseas."

Like an airline standby, you can get on the flight if a seat becomes available. Welcome to the University of Uncertainty: maybe you've been accepted, or maybe you haven't. While you're waiting, the college of your choice is handing out gobs of money to students who were accepted earlier and/or had better GPAs and/or SATs. How much does that leave for you once you're notified that you can come but much of the money's already been allocated?

Hard facts Schools which accept less than 50% of applicants admitted 12.5% off a wait list in 2013; all other schools accepted 29%. Wait lists are more common with private schools than public institutions. And students who express the most interest in getting off the list are more likely to be given a more serious second look. Most colleges want evidence that you're in love with their school.

Even if your student has a near perfect SAT score, a 4.0 GPA, makes singer-guest appearances with the Dallas Symphony, runs a 3-minute mile, and you work 3 jobs to feed your family, you could be passed over by a student with lesser grades, who performed 10 minutes of community service, but whose parents are wealthy. Why? Wealthy parents are the economic heroes to the college that relies on a need-sensitive admissions policy. Money talks and poor students walk. See section, *2 Dirty Secrets*.

Parents with lots of money save these colleges big bucks because they also make large donations to their multi-million dollar endowment funds. The few but growing mega universities with billion-dollar endowments simply show their true school colors: 50 shades of green.

Why would colleges act this way? Not qualifying for aid makes it much easier for the college to embrace you in a flash. It's dream decision-making, the ultimate no-brainer for the college's financial aid office. And the waving flag of economic discrimination continues to fly high on American college campuses.

Such unfairness works hand-in-hand with acceptable racial discrimination (aka "good racism"). If there are 2 affluent students of equal talent and one has a minority-looking name, is there any doubt who gets admitted? This plays oh-so-conveniently into the school's cosmetic diversity. The college ends up giving itself a two-for-one deal: it saves a bundle of cash, and admitting a minority student validates the school's ongoing self-congratulatory and on-your-knees devotion to the god of political correctness. See section, *The Cost Of Diversity.*

What's your strategy? Have an agreement with your child that you will place the college on *your* wait list. If your student is later accepted, wait for the usual follow-up award letter. If the wait-listed school (even if it's not your first choice) offers more financial aid than those schools that accepted your student, use their letter as leverage to get more aid out of your first choice. To be wait-listed could be profitable. One of my students used this tactic and received another $3,000 *per year* in grant money – free bucks!

Attitude check Because of the multitude of colleges to choose from, you don't *need* any particular college. In effect, allow yourself to maintain control of the admissions process instead of surrendering it to a college. Part of your admissions strategy must include the practicality of choosing several other schools where the student can be happy.

Warning to your student: don't overdose on why you want to go to a specific college, only to ignore more than 4,000 other choices. Never allow any college to force your parents to pay top dollar and burden you with more debt after graduation. That would make losers of you both.

Once you have made your final decision on which college to attend, I urge you to contact all the schools that accepted your student and tell them your child isn't coming so that a wait-listed student can have your slot. It could mean someone's hopes being realized and their dreams fulfilled. It's the right thing to do.

Cheaper In Canada
Not Found In US News & World Report

In the movie, *Goodbye Girl*, financially-strapped Richard Dreyfuss wanted to make a great impression on a first date. Before knocking on her door, he walked into a liquor store and blurted out, "Gimme the best, cheapest wine you got!" Some parents have been very impressed to discover that some of the best, cheapest colleges are found in Canada. With its own best schools, the cost can be 1/2 the price of US schools. Here are 3 good examples:

University of Toronto Rated the #1 school in Canada. Its cost in US dollars for international students approximates $44,000 a year with single room and meal plan. America's highest-profile colleges cost between $45,000 and $60,000 a year. The U of T has had "major research achievements such as the discovery of insulin, the creation of the first electronic heart pacemaker, the single lung transplant and the discovery of the gene responsible for the most severe form of Alzheimer's disease." Morley Safer of *60 Minutes* claims Toronto to be the best-designed city in North America. Flight time from Boston to Toronto: 1 hr 38 min; Drive time from Boston, MA to Ithaca College (NY): 6 hrs 30 min. See **Free Travel** on the next page.

Univ of Toronto website: http://www.utoronto.ca

McGill University is an English-language university located in the center of one the largest French-speaking cities in the world. A modern city with a distinctly European flair, Montreal is home for one of Canada's largest universities with almost 30,000 students, offering programs in some 300 disciplines. Cost in US dollars for international students per year: $28,000 with a single room and meal plan. This school, in addition to Brigham Young University in Utah, may be the best value in North America. Flight time from Boston to Montreal: 1 hr 10 min; Drive Time from Boston, MA to Univ of Vermont, 4 hours 36 min

McGill University website: http://www.mcgill.ca

Dalhousie University Located in the heart of eastern Canada's most popular tourist city, Halifax, Nova Scotia. Dalhousie's campus is within walking distance of other colleges, historic sites, and seaside attractions. Students come from all across Canada and over 100 countries. A number of Dalhousie's departments have been ranked among the best in the country. Cost in US dollars: $19,000-23,000/yr with a single room and meal plan. Flight time from Boston to Halifax: 1 hr 25 min; Drive Time from Boston, MA to Villanova (PA): 5 hr 34 min

Dalhousie University website: http://www.dal.ca

Free Travel With higher gasoline prices, you can fly FREE to and from these schools if you get one of those airline credit cards. They allow you to earn bonus miles on purchases made at gas stations, supermarkets, home improvement and hardware stores, drugstores, U.S. Post Office, and how about this? - paying for college! You'll feel right at home when these colleges have you fill out the standard FAFSA form for financial aid.

It's a good time to look north of the border. It's a proven way to win the college money game.

"How can anyone rationally argue that a baseball player should get a college scholarship, but a piano player shouldn't? What does it say about a college's regard for art, literature, drama and music if the finest young painters, writers, actors and musicians are not eligible for the same rewards as are athletes?"

Frank Deford
Senior Writer, Sports Illustrated

Outside The Mainstream
Special Groups Get Help

Separated or Divorced Parents

1. The financial aid forms should be completed by the parent with whom the student lives for 6 months and one day of the year. For example, if a child lives with his mother for 9 months out of the year and with his father only 3 months, the income and asset information will be based on the mother only.

2. If the parent with whom the child resides is remarried, you must include the income and the assets of the stepparent as if he or she were the biological parent. This may not sound fair, but this is the way the financial aid formulas work.

3. Private colleges and universities can ask to see the income and asset information of the non-custodial parent when awarding their own funds. With the CSS Profile - a private college's favorite lethal weapon against you - wants to ask about the income and assets of the non-custodial parent, you can choose to respond or not respond. After all, you can consider yourself the scrutinized and victimized parent. If you choose *not* to respond to any of their inquiries, they'll be pressed to make a decision on the student's aid package without fully knowing your financial picture. They'll make an uninformed decision because you did not give them anything to see; colleges do this all the time. Legally, you're clear. And the student could gain from your position because the colleges will err on the side of the student who cannot be held responsible for separation or divorce issues.

4. If you want to take a tax deduction as the non-custodial parent, and you're wondering if it will matter, here's the bad news: a tax deduction is a non-issue to the schools when awarding financial aid in custodial cases. The schools don't care who takes the tax deduction; that's strictly a tax issue between the parents.

Here's the issue for financial aid: the parent whose income is less and has the child living in the same domicile stands to get more financial aid. But if your daughter, for example, is living with you and you make more money, she gets less financial aid. If you're making less money than the student's other parent, and she's living with you, she qualifies for more aid.

Here's the ideal situation for getting the most financial aid (not for taxes): the student lives with the parent who makes less money. Period. End of story. That parent fills out the FAFSA form as the custodial parent. The student now qualifies for more financial aid.

Here's the ideal situation for a better tax situation (not for financial aid): the parent claiming the child as a dependent gets a tax advantage. If the student is living with the parent who's making less money, but the non-custodial parent is claiming her as a dependent, both parents win: the student gets more aid, and the non-custodial parent gets a tax deduction.

Although most financial aid is based on "need," financial aid packages are based to some extent on how much colleges want your child. There are some "special interest" groups:

Academic Superstars
Many schools try to attract top students away from the more highly-rated schools by offering academic scholarships. If your child is academically gifted, use this as a bargaining chip. This is how millionaires with talented kids get FREE money.

Athletes
Division #2 or #3 schools offer preferential packaging (more grants, less loans) to attract your child to their school even if s/he is not qualified for Division #1. Meet the coach at each school you visit. Get the high school coach to write letters of recommendation to Division 1 schools, and have the coach contact the college's coach to brag about your student.

Minorities
Find out about the availability of scholarship programs for minorities, which of course are clearly, unmistakably and unambiguously unfair to achievement-proven majority students.

Owning Your Own Business
If you currently own your own business, or you're thinking of starting one, there are significant benefits when it comes to getting money for college. For example, the net value of a business with less than 100 employees is not counted on the FAFSA form, a fact that's relevant only if your kid is going to a school that doesn't require the CSS Profile. Also, you have the ability to control (or lower) your income during the years that your child is in college,

thereby making you eligible for more financial aid. See section, **Start A Business Now.**

Recently Unemployed

If you were recently terminated, or have received notice that you will be terminated, or if you own your own business and cannot make a living due to current economic conditions, you must make the college financial aid officer aware of this immediately.

For special circumstances there is something called "Professional Judgment" that a financial aid officer can use to help you out in tough situations. To request it can be very productive.

Independent Students Six criteria determine independent status: (1) twenty-four years of age or older before Dec 31st of their first year of college; (2) armed forces vet; (3) an orphan or ward of the court; (4) have legal dependents; (5) a graduate or professional student; and (6) married. If your child doesn't fit into one of the above criteria, your request for financial aid probably won't fly. But here's where it will fly...

Illegal Aliens This in-your-face phenomenon drives my clients bonkers. Currently 16 states are violating federal law (Title 8, Chapter 14, Sec 1623 of the US Code) by allowing the same in-state fees at state schools for the students of illegal aliens. If you're an American-born parent who speaks English, works hard, obeys the law and pays taxes, and your child attends a state school that's out-of-state, an illegal alien could easily enjoy paying half of your rate. Here are the states where out-of-country, non-citizen, and legal-age law-breakers get a big break on tuition fees at USA state schools from tax-paying and born-in-the-USA citizens: Connecticut, Colorado, Florida, Maryland, Minnesota, Nebraska, New Jersey, New Mexico, Texas, New York, Oregon, California, Washington, Utah, Illinois, and Kansas.

Moral of this story? Crime pays for law-breakers in law-breaking states.

How Students Flunk In
Is Flunking Out A Thing Of The Past?

Ever hear of a college student flunking OUT of a $60,000-a-year college? No? Ever wonder why? Because the student's parents are an ATM machine: it empties the parents' required amount into the school's coffers every month like clockwork. What business would mess with success?

If your student is doing badly from your perspective, you can rest assured that the college has a different point of view. It's not likely to shut you down. That's called Flunking IN. Your student gets to stay IN school. And you get to marvel at the school's generosity of tolerance for underachievers. Or, you've resigned yourself to the reality that there's no such thing as "educational malpractice."

"And it's not just the colleges that are implicated in this," says Patrick M. Callan, President of the National Center for Public Policy & Higher Education. "Most states fund higher education based on how many students they enroll. So if a student drops out, and they can put another one in that seat the next day or the next quarter, there's no consequence for the college, in terms of the public accountability."

If your student doesn't get the grades to justify your expense, they can marvel at your intolerance for mediocrity or failure. Then it's time to transfer to the school of hard knocks, where your child can live the joy of repeating over fifty times a day, "Would you like fries with that?"

When my first offspring decided not to attend an art class and received an F grade, he remembers my warning him that a repetition of an F grade meant my helping him pack his bags and coming home for good. I made it crystal clear that there was no such thing as a parental subsidy for failure. To this day he declares that it was the most motivating email he ever read in college. It was my own version of flunking IN, the only version I recommend.

College Money Traps
After Your Student Shows Up

To get more of your money in the college game, colleges and universities are like mosquitoes at a backyard barbecue: they'll nickel-and-dime you to distraction, especially if your child's a 1st-year student. The following examples say it all:

1. Paper & Parking Copies from an ordinary copy machine can cost 15 cents a page (U Connecticut) when a typical print shop charges less. My son can purchase $450 worth of books for his next semester for $190 on the internet, but college bookstores happily charge full price. Pay a $10 fine for the first time you're caught without a parking sticker; $30 for the third time; or, $50 for the fifth time (U Massachusetts/Dartmouth). Parking violations are such a big business that many colleges relish the thought of having hundreds of 1st-year students with cars on campus.

2. Lost & Late Pay $25 to replace your lost student ID (Fitchburg State University). A late book return to the library, after a grace period, can mean a fine of $25 per book per day (Boston College). Late decisions on course selections can cost $25 (U New Hampshire). If you're late in dropping a class after a deadline, it can cost you $600 (Worcester State University). Or, a private college will still charge you the full semester's tuition - with no refund - if you drop a course whose pro-rated value is $4,200 (Boston U). Watch $35 fly out of your wallet when you replace your room key (Clark U).

3. Picky & Petty Your student checks out a computer from the computer lab. Not noticing that anything is missing, the computer is returned without its canvas case. Your student is hit quickly with the meaning of a 20-dollar deficit. But there was no canvas case in the first place. There was no record signed as to the condition of the borrowed item. You lose. Or, each of the library computers has a small sticker that notifies the user not to use the computer for email. If caught, you're fined. Watch those hardly-noticeable installment fees - could be 1.5% of your total. Or, the extra $1,000 for health insurance you don't need. Here's a nightmare from one student: "I didn't realize that if I dropped a class after the 5th instructional day it would count toward termination of my financial aid."

Colleges hide behind the firewall that protects them from the most stressed bill-payers - parents - who do not have to be notified about what the student forgets, or ignores. Instead, being of legal age, it's the student's responsibility (read: because students pay little or no attention, the parents will pay). If the student is a freshman, that's when the parent is most vulnerable. Your freshman may have this mindset: "Rules? What rules?!" Eighteen year-olds, away from controlling parents for the first time, are easily tempted to ignore rules. Because this fact is life-sustaining oxygen to the colleges, they carefully set their profit-center traps and place them all over campus. Sooner or later, your student will step in one. Kaching!

When does it end? Never. The so-called "real world" started the day your student showed up. To add insult to injury, colleges don't wait for your student to graduate: they want contributions from you now. Like death and taxes, solicitations are guaranteed until death. Actually, even after death.

What to do? Both parent and student should have a copy of the college's calendar of deadlines and campus rule book. They are the gold standards used by the colleges to get your gold. Write personal letters with documentation to reverse unreasonable fee charges. Read your bills carefully - mistakes happen. Most of all, with patience, be a real pain.

Don't bother reminding the college of the most sacred rule in marketing: the customer is always right. They don't believe it for a second.

"What remains of the '60s on our campuses are its worst sides: intolerance of dissent,...the self-appointed power...to set everyone else's moral agenda, and, saddest of all, the belief that universities not only may but should suspend the rights of some in order to transform students, the culture, and the nation according to their ideological vision and desire."

Alan Charles Kors & Harvey A. Silverglate
The Shadow University, from the Introduction

6 Survival Tips
First 6 Weeks Of College

My clients with entering college freshman receive this masterpiece of tips. More college freshmen will drop out of college in the first 6 weeks than at any other time this year (53% will drop out after the first year). But the 6 tips below have proven to work, according to Dr. R. Gilbert of Montclair State University in New Jersey:

1. Treat your roommates like they're your best friends...even if they aren't.

2. Never assume anything...no matter what your question. Keep asking until 2 people give you the same exact answer.

3. No matter what your problem...there is an expert on campus to help you. First, check with your Head of Residence. Then, go to the Dean of Students office.

4. Don't be intimidated. College *looks* much more difficult than it really is.

5. When you think everyone else is so much smarter than you, remember this quote: "College is a fountain of knowledge. A few come to drink, a few come to sip, and, unfortunately, the rest come to gargle."

6. When you feel like dropping out, repeat slowly this question several times:

"Would you like fries with that?"

This last one gets a laugh, but it's no joke. Like the condemned man about to be executed, it forces a student to focus on what's really important.

Why Pay An Expert?
A National Group's Big Bamboozle

An experienced financial aid specialist knows where the college's gold is hidden, and smart parents know it's worth paying an expert to get some of it. Private colleges don't fear that you're going to hire someone who finds the gold. Why? Because these experts are so few and hard to find, which means very few parents will use them. And besides, colleges are too arrogant to care.

But financial aid administrators who have their own organization, the National Association of Student Financial Aid Administrators, want to warn you about these experts. It's the classic story of the elephant fearing the mouse. Since an administrator's expertise is a one-note song telling you how and where to get more loans to afford college, here's their never-ending mantra, their unabashed advisory statement on their website (www.nasfaa.org) as of this writing: "Before considering a consultant, first speak to a financial aid administrator."

It's the equivalent of suggesting that, should you need your car engine repaired, you should go to a young kid who only pumps gas, instead of speaking to an experienced mechanic at the same service station. In other words, this group would have you believe that both occupations are equivalent, one is as good as the other, and that both can perform the same functions. Even though both are in the same work area, their areas of expertise are worlds apart. This group can't resist barking: "A financial aid administrator can perform these same services [of a consultant] free of charge."

Same services? What we have is this group's...

Big Bamboozle They list 5 functions that suggest a match to exactly what they do: preparing the FAFSA, estimating your resources, your EFC, your financial need, and "the types of federal, state, local and institutional aid programs that are available." But they don't perform 4 out of the 5 functions themselves. They only perform the 5th function: their purpose is to describe "the types of federal, state, local and institutional aid programs that are available." They do a good job of it. But it would appear that they want you to believe the list they contrived is all we experts do. It's not a "misstatement," not a "false statement," but a bamboozle.

Financial Aid Experts There aren't enough of them, and this association would have you think that the experts are kids at the gas pump. Experts do more than paperwork; they provide valuable information on how to appropriate aid from colleges for families who qualify for aid, and how to use tax-favored devices to afford college for families who don't qualify for need-based aid. Parents and students have saved thousands of dollars with such information, and have gladly paid for it. Financial aid administrators won't accept that they are the kids at the pump, and their website's whoppers do an enormous injustice not only to this tiny group of experts, but more importantly to the financially-burdened parents who need and want them.

College Admission Experts By contrast these experts do not engage the financial process exclusively but instead concentrate on placing students into the right-fit colleges, schools that are affordable for the parents and academically- and socially-matched to the student. Which is what I do. By contrast, I'm suspicious of college financial "experts" who simply sell life insurance policies and annuities to families as ways to qualify for more financial aid. Independent admission advisors have as their primary focus the student's needs without ignoring the financial needs of the parents. The ultimate goal is a right-fit college for both parent and student. To learn more of my coaching and marketing strategies that get my students into their first choice colleges, which their parents can afford, visit my website:

www.planningforcollege.net

"...we are finding that grade inflation is... symptomatic of a larger problem which someone described as 'a mutual non-aggression pact' between teacher and student: don't ask much of me, and I won't ask much of you."

John Merrow

College Early Action
And Christmas

What happens when a student is accepted on this basis?

Validation! For once the student is feeling "accepted" for who s/he is, not for what everyone else has been claiming for years. Because some "institution" has said, "Congrats! You're in," it has validated the student in ways they never imagined.

"I did it!" is what I hear from my students at this time of year, and colleges who are smart enough to send out acceptance letters to Early Action applicants just before Christmas Day are doing the student and themselves an excellent service: the student is feeling ecstatic before the biggest holiday of the year, and the college is looking like an academic Santa Claus to the parents and the student.

Ego Boost: Any announcement of acceptance is a huge ego boost for a 17-year-old. And we all can use an ego boost from time to time. But this is a very special boost: it says the student has value, the kind that tells the student that your value has a great deal of weight with us, and we're looking forward to seeing your value on our campus.

If your child is accepted to any college before Christmas Day, this is the time to celebrate to the max!

Study Abroad?
Advice I Gave To Two Students

Below is a letter I sent to two of my college-coaching students who are sisters, who decided they wanted to attend college outside of the United States.

Dear Eva and Lily,

I am thrilled to learn that the both of you will be attending the College of Saint Andrews this fall. You have made a decision that will influence your life in ways that you cannot imagine even now. But I'll give you a hint as to how. Right here.

By attending college outside of the country can be viewed as a metaphor for thinking "outside the box." People who do such thinking discover horizons in their future that others cannot see, or are simply unwilling to leave open the possibilities that's there's a window through which greater possibilities can be seen. It's their comfort zone that forces them to remain where they are, and we've heard time and again that real growth for any of us is to live outside our comfort zones – to see, hear, feel, and taste things we never knew existed.

Put another way, staying close to home as a new college student is like a new ship staying in harbor. But a ship isn't built for the purpose of staying in harbor. Its purpose is to ride the sometimes stormy seas where adventure, excitement, and the discovery of new worlds exist. And your growth will be the expansion of those horizons that started you on your life voyage with your decision to step outside your comfort zones.

As you live outside of your country, you will be exposed to cultures and ideas unfamiliar to you. By the time graduation comes, you will have walked through the Louvre in Paris, Westminster Abbey in London, the Sistine Chapel in Rome, not to mention coming to know individuals who grew up and lived in the environments that made these experiences real for you. In other words, you will experience and internalize realities that you would never experience at any college in the United States.

And how do you place a price-tag on those experiences? You don't. You can't.

You will return home in four years with a perspective that is wider and deeper than anyone else your age. You will raise the bar of expectations from future employers who will only be too happy to meet them, and the quality of the gentlemen you allow to pursue you will be of a quality to match your own. Not a bad additional benefit that will last a lifetime.

When you enter the job-interview-after-college phase of your life, it will become obvious to any future employer that you are a very special individual. And the question you will likely hear at the end of your interviews is , "When can you start?"

Your parents are to be commended for their support of your decision. Typically, parents are unintentional co-conspirators in having their children remain in their comfort zones, they simply find a convenient way to keep you close, not wanting to let go. It's only natural. It's so difficult for a parent to see their children leave home forever, but your parents are stepping outside their comfort zones so that you can begin to enrich yours. And it's a sacrifice they are making that reflects one of the most difficult support-decisions I believe they have ever made. But they put you before themselves in a way that most parents cannot handle. They are pretty special, just as their daughters are.

As with all my students, it's been an honor for me to have served you in my small way, and it's been a thrill to have been a part of your process in applying to college.

My most sincere congratulations to you and your parents for a great and far-reaching decision.

It's time to acknowledge the following: You're the best.

How To Pay For College
Here Are Plans B, C, D, And E

If you don't have a Plan B, let's start here...

Plan A: A high school senior found her right-fit school, that is, it was the right size, the right lattes, the right ambiance, the right major, the right geography, the right mascot, and even a right financial aid package that left her struggling parents with an out-of-pocket expense of $14,500 at a $45,000-a-year school.

I say "struggling" parents because $14,500 was still hard to materialize, but they said they'd find a way, whatever that meant. But out of nowhere, a wrong-fit college sent the student a free application, and on a whim the student submitted it. The college came back with a financial aid package that left the parents with a total out-of-pocket cost of $2,900.

A no-brainer, right?

After the first semester, the student announces that she really doesn't like her college and wants to transfer. The parents are in a panic: the remaining three years of grants, worth a total of $75,000, are down the tubes.

Almost spasmodically, the student applies to three private schools in the same league as the school she wants to leave, naively assuming that she would receive the same financial aid package that she was leaving behind. Only one of the private colleges offers her a $5,000 grant, but the parents have to come up with another $42,000. Can't be done.

Now what? The following are more ways to pay for college:

1. Plan B: She can stay where she is and "gut it out," meaning, she can stay in a liberal arts curriculum with the intent of developing her thinking, writing, and communication skills for any profession. This is not unrealistic, despite how idealistic it may look; it can be argued that college is for developing, nurturing, and maximizing communication skills.

2. Plan C: She can come home, lose her remaining three years of grants worth $75,000 (ouch!), and find a no-skills-necessary job in a downward economy. Good luck.

3. Plan D: She can transfer to a near-home community college and use a Stafford loan to pay for her second year of college, get her core courses out of the way, and with no financial obligation from the parents in the second year of college. Then, with a degree from a community college, she can transfer to an in-state state college for a lot less money than what she would pay at any of the private colleges to which she applied.

4. Plan E: She can bypass the community college choice and transfer to an in-state state college where the parents' out-of-pocket costs stay under $10,000.

Even though Plan A and B's $75,000 in grants are lost, it can mean an opportunity to get a college education at a very affordable price.

Economically, private schools simply don't have the appeal they once had. Realism's ugly face is causing parents and students to make choices that were not so hard after all, and one of the above plans can turn out to be very positive.

Scholarships Out Of Nowhere

$400 For Completing An Application?

The University of Rochester pulled back the curtain on how it awards a merit scholarship. For example, your student gets a $400 discount (read: "scholarship") for completing his/her college application. And how about receiving $62 for every "A" that's on a student's transcript? Forget that your child is a long way from being a national merit scholar.

I think the University of Rochester's revelation indicated just how prominent is the human factor in the awarding of merit aid. In other words, grades and test scores are obvious criteria for awarding a merit scholarship, but it's not the "standard" criteria, that is, aid based strictly on the academic achievement evidenced in the college admissions application. Here's what got most of my attention from the Dean's comments:

"Admitted students who had serious conversations with admissions and financial aid counselors earned $3,000 average difference in merit aid. Even before admission, students who scheduled a recommended admissions interview earned on average $250 more in merit."

In other words, *direct personal contact* can mean a merit scholarship. What's that got to do with merit? Nothing. *It has everything to do with human relationships*. Could this be a "reality check" on how to get a merit scholarship, a job, a promotion?

Can we agree that relationships make a difference in our daily transactions? To advance our cause – any cause, we know that using our voice boxes can generate a faster and more welcome response. That's showing up versus texting or emailing.

Naturally each college assigns its own dollar amounts to whatever your student does to be admitted. I like the looks of $3,000 and $250 for having a "serious conversation" with someone in admissions.

One of my wealthiest students last year, who met no criteria for merit aid on the college's website, had that conversation and was awarded a $5,000 merit scholarship.

I couldn't prove that my tight choreography of that conversation had anything to do with it, but you couldn't convince the parents that it didn't. This University of Rochester study – here comes my shameless and self-serving point – offers the validation of my technique that has prompted me to write this.

Something as small as the *Thank You* note may not generate a dime in a merit scholarship, but the mind-set that writes that note stands a better chance of getting something that may come from totally out of nowhere.

College Costs Going Higher?
Good!

College costs are too high; that's good. Why? It forces parents to be realistic about college choices; that's better. And students will learn some real life-lessons as a result of making hard choices; that's best.

There may be more heart-break about where kids are going to college. Let's talk about the elephant in the room that's making a lot of noise, but parents would like to ignore: the growing cost of college.

When I start working with a client, here's the first question I ask: "What is the *absolute* limit you will spend on your child's college education?" I force people to focus on money from the get-go. Otherwise, I hear in-sane statements like, "I want my daughter to enjoy the same college experience I had."

Yeah, I'd like to own a Rolls Royce, but I can't afford it. Parents are still stuck in the tortured idealism of paying for college "somehow," even though they haven't saved a dime for college.

Here's my standard anecdote on how students are being misled.

"Sweetheart, work hard and do all the things your guidance counselor tells you and you can go to any college."

Does this read familiar? It's garbage, and parents are feeding it to their kids everyday and deluding themselves at the same time.

To the point: Our students are not getting the right impressions about college, let alone having a discussion about college, which is usually done on the fly; however, that engagement is changing. Recently, I spent an hour on a Skype call with a family in California, and the one word the student continued to use was "prestige."

Where did that word "prestige" come from? From her parents, her teachers, her classmates, and worst of all, from people in my industry who should know better.

It's like a well-meaning but unintended conspiracy against the student who shouldn't be hearing this nonsense. And I proceeded to tell the student in front of her Ivy League-grad parents that prestige won't buy you a can of Bull in this day and culture.

When I explained why the Ivys no longer have the "prestige" any more, (See the following chapter) the parents were actually relieved. Before the call was done, the student thought it just made more sense to go to the local state university and *not* to Stanford where she would come out with $100,000 of debt. The difference in debt for this student was going to be $16,000 versus $100,000. This is a REAL choice.

Parents, classmates and high school officials are totally misinforming these kids who are put under stress to succeed and excel, much of which – ready for this? – is to make the high schools look good and for many parents to validate themselves through their children. It's unconscionable, but some people's priorities adversely affect these students. When they don't get into their so-called "prestige" schools, the disappointment can be humiliating and demoralizing.

The hard-working students deserve real information that makes sense so that debt is not on their horizon. The politicians in DC can't handle debt, but you can. And it begins by making common-sense choices where the word "prestige" will be heard as a dirty word (I "get it" that there's an exception to every rule, but the realities of our economy don't allow for the luxury of embracing the exception).

If you want to do yourself and your child a huge favor, use these reality themes: Go to a school and educate yourself; no one is going to educate you but you; no college makes you succeed – you make yourself succeed. And you can provide your own themes, I'm sure.

Your student deserves better than the abbreviated motivational outbursts ("You can do it!") from teachers and friends, and it begins with your being realistic with them right from the start. The end result is a Charlie Sheen moment: "Duh! Winning!" (Sorry, I couldn't help myself!)

Ivy League Colleges

Why They're Irrelevant

They don't mean much any more. They're known as being "prestige" colleges and "elite" colleges. But only to people who like to write about them. In this political climate where long-held requirements for political office are being tossed overboard, its ripple effect is growing to be a tsunami. It's over, Ivys. You can no longer take "prestige" and "elite" to the bank. Such terms are now bankrupt of meaning. And it's about time.

In marketing, as the saying goes, perception is reality. American business has grown to believe - fairly or unfairly - that students attending the Ivys grow up in a bubble of privilege and graduate in a bubble of entitlement. A Gallup poll in 2013 concluded that 91% of American business leaders place little importance on where a student attends college, but instead prefer a grad who has some knowledge of the expertise being sought and has good communication skills.

The arrogance astounds.

Every May these colleges love to remind us how many applicants they reject, as if telling the world that rejecting talented students is a redeeming quality to be advertised. They don't get it: nobody really cares about their statistics, that they have large armies of teaching assistants masquerading as faculty, and if your student wants an appointment with a famous professor, forget it – he doesn't talk to undergrads. You can find this information in a well-researched book (***Higher Education?***) that's partly written by an Ivy League professor (I wonder if she still has her job…).

Wall Street Journal (Online, Sept 13, 2010, Teri Evans)

It's a well-established fact that companies are now recruiting grads from big state universities instead of going after the Ivy grads. Why? One conclusion was stated this way: "Recruiters say graduates of top public universities are often among the most prepared and well-rounded academically, the WSJ said. Companies have found they fit well into their corporate cultures and over time have the best track record in their firms."

My conclusion?

The Ivys costs a whole lot more and deliver a whole lot less. Period.. And the Ivys are too arrogant to notice or care. After all, there are enough parents out there who don't get it either.

College Double Major

Waste Of Effort, Time And Money

What happens when you're working on two projects at the same time? Both take longer to complete, and under tight time constraints you cannot focus all your attention on getting one project done right or on time. That pretty much sums up what students are doing with a double major.

Waste of Effort

There is no evidence in the job market that employers are looking for college grads who double-majored. None. All that the student proves is that work came in a greater quantity, which doesn't mean you worked more conscientiously. You had to put in a lot more effort just to get the credits, but where did these credits get you? More knowledge? Or knowledge for knowledge's sake? If you're philosophical and financially capable, it works. Otherwise, it was too much work for little or nothing in return in a hard-bitten world that isn't philosophical.

Waste of Money

Students like to impress me with saying that they want to double-major, as if to suggest they are real achievers. They usually are, but no one is being realistic with them to suggest that focusing on a major and a minor is less expensive. Or that both a major and a minor can give an achieving student what they're looking for, and with less work and for less money. Why less money? Because at a private college, for example, where the parents may pay over $5,000 for a three-credit course – ka-ching! – they may have to fork over another $30,000 – ka-ching! – to pay for those extra courses to earn that double-major distinction. Okay, you got two batchelor's degrees. But at what cost and to what advantage in the job market? Quantity is not quality unless you're killing more of the enemy in combat.

Waste of Time

Nearly 70% of all college grads finish college after five or six years. You can bet a lot of double-majors are in this group. Students didn't really know what they wanted to major in, so they hedged their bets by staying in college longer. Ka-ching! Time is money, which is a truism students are not likely to hear from an economics professor who never owned a business. Theories can be expensive.

Recommendation

Have your student take a Myers-Briggs and Strong personality assessment to give focus and direction to your student, something you wish you had when you were seventeen years old. It's a start, and it's foundational with everything I do with my students who want to get into the right-fit major at the right-fit college.

The Appeal Letter
How To Write It

Colleges overcharge. This is the operative assumption you must operate with when dealing with the college "award" letter, which is nothing more than the bill. The top half of the letter will list - in deadpan fashion – what discounts (read: scholarships and/or grants) and loans your student will receive; the bottom half will announce, with the harmony of steroid-pumped singing angels, what you have to pay.

Your friends will treat the letter as a polished stone tablet. "Gee, all my kid is getting is a $2,000 grant and a bunch of loans. Now what?" The recipient never thinks that the "award" can be altered by appealing it. Fitting the colleges' contemptuous stereotype of parents as "dummies," it's only logical that a parent will pick up the phone and start dialing financial institutions that sell student loans.

Let's just bypass the headaches that come with not knowing what to do and get down to my magic formula that does NOT work every time, but does work in most instances.

The following is based on the premise that your student has applied to a lot of colleges. I have all my client-students apply to *at least* ten colleges, which makes educators wince or gag at the suggestion. But I will state my case, and you be the judge.

Your daughter applied to ten colleges, and the offers are coming in. She likes her top five very much, and three have given her sizable discounts, otherwise called "scholarships" and "grants." But her first choice's offer is $3,000 less than the other two. With the presumption that each of these three schools are in the same league (same GPA and test requirements), you can use the other two offers as ammunition against the first-choice.

The language must be crafted carefully. Here's what you don't say: "Because the economy sucks..." Such indelicate verbiage may get a few laughs, but you don't want a financial aid counselor laughing at your request. Plus, stating the obvious about the economy will get you nowhere because every "dummy" is saying so in *their* appeal letters. By NOT saying so already establishes the high credibility of your appeal. All you have to do now is validate it.

Here comes the fun part.

Figure your POOP score (my very own acronym for Parent-Out-Of-Pocket money). If the first-choice college is going to cost you more than the other two, say so. Refer but do NOT provide evidence from the other two offers just yet. Make the colleges ask for it because they may; they want to see if you're bluffing. Even if they say "no" to your request without asking for evidence, your response is the same: ignore their response and your second correspondence will provide copies of the other schools' offers. Tah-dah! You just threw the ball in their court with titanic evidence they can't ignore, and now they have to do something with it. They won't fumble, and you can't either.

Let's say they come back with a negative response. Now what? Send back the last correspondence with a note that says, "Perhaps I wasn't clear in my request for help. Unless you can help me with a little more money, I will be forced to consider my other choices very soon." Enclose copies of the other colleges' offers again. Notice I did not suggest anything with finality, as in "I won't attend if you don't give me what I want." This is *sucking up* time, and you'd better be good at it.

The ball is back in their court again. BTW, never accept a college's statement that says, "Our offer is non-negotiable." That is atomic and sub-atomic baloney. All offers are negotiable. It's an intimidating statement that dummies accept, something colleges are counting on. The college may come back and match the offer of your first-choice. You win. This scenario works often, but not all the time. It depends on the school's available discounts they can give, the economy (!), their dwindling endowments, your timing, or increase in donors this year, whatever. You simply cannot tell from year to year.

The magic formula is simple: ASK, an acronym for "Ask and you shall receive, Seek and you shall find, and Knock and it will be opened to you." What did you teach your kids all these years? If you don't ask, you don't get.

I understand there are other scenarios that don't fit what you just read, and space doesn't allow me to continue. But the best advice I can give you is to use the formula, and never use negative statements in your appeal. Ask for help, not for money, and reiterate that you're looking forward to attending if the appeal can be met. *And have your student sign the letter.*

How To Graduate In 3 Years
And Save A Ton Of Money

How does a student finish college in 3 years, and what are the advantages of doing so? Here's how:

1. Take as many Advanced Placement (AP) or International Baccalaureate (IB) classes as possible in high school. These are college courses for which you will get college credit as long as you score a 4 or better (maximum is 5) on the AP exam. If for some reason you were shut out of these courses, go to a local community college, or better yet, a local private college with more competitive rates; Dean College in Franklin, MA is a very good example of a private college whose credits are accepted everywhere, and whose costs are more competitive. Always verify that the credits you receive will indeed be accepted at the college you will be attending.

2. Take advantage of the free time during school breaks. The Christmas break, for example, can last as long as 5 weeks. Many colleges will offer, say, a ten-day course during this break, and a student can pick up another 3 credits. Let's do the math: 3 credits X 3 Christmas breaks = 9 credits. Courses can also be taken nights and on weekends.

3. The summer is an ideal time to pick up another two courses. If your student starts out with one course between the junior and senior years – to test-drive the college experience - and then takes two courses each summer until they are juniors in college, that's 3 credits before the high school senior year, 6 credits per summer for the next 3 summers = 21 credits. Total so far = 30. You need 120 credits to graduate, and you knocked off one-fourth of those credits. You're done in three years! Bam! Since summer breaks can last as long as fifteen weeks, these summer courses are only six weeks long, or they can be four weeks long. Hardly an inconvenience during vacation time.

4. Take online courses at the college you already attend. By contrast, do not take an online course with another college because your own school cannot prove that you actually did the work. It's safer to stick with your own college. If you want to do otherwise, verify with your college that they will accept credit for such online courses from another college.

5. Take CLEP tests. These are tests that allow you to test out of a college course. For roughly the cost of a study manual ($20) and the registration fee ($80), you can earn college credit at most colleges and save yourself as much as $4,000 per course. That's a-w-e-s-o-m-e! Top tier schools don't give credit for these tests, but you can contact the CollegeBoard website, whose profile of each school will tell you whether or not the college allows for CLEP credit.

6. Gut it out. Here's my favorite anecdote to getting a degree in three years: one of my clients told me that she finished in three years because her father told her: "You'll have to graduate in three years because I only have enough money to pay for three." Not one to question her father at seventeen, she loaded up on courses every semester and finished in three years with honors. She took no courses during semester breaks or during the summer time. Her father lied about the money he had.

What are the advantages? Save money! How?

1. Here's a real-life example of a savings for completing in three years: Stonehill College in Easton, MA is a highly ranked private college whose costs are roughly $58,000 a year. They charge $1,285 per credit, compared to UMass/Boston's $72 per credit; that's a difference of $1,213.00. If you're a student at Stonehill who's going to get 30 credits at UMass/Boston that are transferrable to Stonehill, you saved – here's the math – 30 credits X $1.213/per credit savings = $36,390 saved. But wait! The student didn't spend a 4th year at Stonehill, thereby saving the parents another $21,610 ($58,000 minus $38,390 already saved). Sweet! Put down this book, stand up, raise your hands above your head, and scream, "YES!"

2. When you finish college and create your resume, you will be sending the following signals to prospective employers: I'm ambitious, I'm industrious, I'm not afraid to work hard, I have the ideal work ethic you're looking for, I understand the meaning of the word "sacrifice," I don't have an attitude of entitlement, and I'm an expert at – no surprise – time management.

3. Your interview advantage will be huge. Just on the surface, you will likely be a positive curiosity, that is, the only applicant for the position you seek who finished college in three years. Unheard of!

4. You will be in the work force one year earlier. That's probably a gain of at least $35,000 to your life-time earnings. Or, in this economy, where inexpensive inexperience trumps expensive experience, you're likely to get hired before most college grads. Additional signal: I'm very competitive.

5. Because college is often a family affair with younger brothers and sisters, you'll be helping them by your sacrifice of time so they get the same chance you received. Plus, you'll be an inspiration to your siblings. And what price do you put on inspiration?

To make this all happen, pretend the economy isn't going to get any better. Act offensively: do what has to be done if the worse happens. And plan your strategy like crazy. And you'll be the richer for it in more ways than one.

Facebook And The Colleges
Rejection Made More Likely

A parent hired me to coach her son on getting into his first-choice college. He appeared to be the ideal student: conscientious, hard-working, achieving, and most noticeably, very polite. I was very impressed.

When I got back to my office the first thing I did was look at his Facebook account. That's because a lot of colleges are doing the same thing before deciding on an applicant's college application.

To my incredible surprise (my naiveté is showing), his opening page was peppered with the "F Bomb" like giant croutons on a salad. Ouch! Immediately I picked up the phone and asked, "Has your mother seen your Facebook page?" His response was pure teenager: "Are you serious?"

I told him he had to sanitize his Facebook like he was cleaning foul-odor garbage from his room. He had a problem with my analogy, but he made it through my logic after several more attempts to explain what I thought was the obvious.

Lesson: Never assume smart high school students are undisputedly socially-aware; they're not.

In short, colleges are using the internet to find another reason to accept or reject an applicant. They're going to the social networks like Facebook. Why? Because that's where *they* spend a lot of *their* time. Admission counselors have lots of friends on *their* Facebook pages.

It's a known fact that users spend at least an hour a day on Facebook; teens at least three hours. So the logical next step is to see if the student is on Facebook. And why not? It's convenient, the admissions officer is already on his own Facebook page. Why not put in the student's name while he's already there? Voila! Revelation!

As a parent, you can snoop your child's Facebook page without them knowing it. Yeah, I know the privacy mechanisms allow you to keep people out of your pages, but 17-year-olds are still naive enough to not use these buttons: "Nah! Nobody check this stuff!"

If you discover what I call "Digital Dirt," suggest that your child use the Ultimate Technology Cleaner: the delete button.

Making your Facebook pages look wholesome is just one of the strategies I use with my own students. It focuses on one single objective: getting in with a clean college application.

How To Get Into College
It's All About "Presentation"

Urgent

Print out the following quotation and post it all over the house for both you and your student to see at least forty times a day:

"I have found that there is one little word that can make the difference between being accepted to a university, being put on the waiting list, and being denied admission: *Presentation*." Kevin M. Hatgas, Asst Dir Admissions, John Carroll University

Key to Success

Ask a student how he got his summer job. Listen carefully to the answer. Try to hear some connection to GRADES. You won't. Which is my point. The employer hired your child based on how s/he came across, how they presented themselves, and amazingly, the employer never asked about their grades. Because grades are irrelevant.

Definition of Presentation

What do I mean by presentation? Submitting a perfect application (read: perfect spelling and capitalization), getting a letter of recommendation that reads like a story instead of a laundry list of personal characteristics, an essay that shows evidence that Spellcheck was used, etc., etc., etc.

Act now.

Now print out the above quote and good luck!

Advice before College

Before my students go off to college, I give them one last piece of advice: No matter what you major in, be absolutely certain that you take a course in marketing. Ask the professor of that course to do a project on how to market YOU. Because for the rest of your life, all you will do is market yourself to prospective employers, customers, groups, organizations and even to your future spouse. All of life revolves around two activities: buying and selling. And marketing is the vehicle for selling yourself for all to buy.

Biggest Mistake
In Choosing a College

Nothing drives me more crazy than watching a parent and a guidance department in concert (read: in a well-intentioned conspiracy) to drive a student in the direction of certain colleges that don't even fit what the student needs.

Here are the good intentions: the student needs to go to a "good" school, which is usually defined by where the parent went to school or where associates of the mom and dad went to school. You know…all that homogenized networking stuff that comes after graduation. As if to suggest that the student needs a crutch upon graduation before making the "Big Time" on his or her own. Or, the parents think their student is smarter than they were at seventeen, and the parents want their college-bound student to aim higher than where they went to college. Is this looking familiar? Is this getting *old* yet? Nope. Not at all, as we discover…

The guidance department is equally handicapped as the parent, both of whom don't have the time to do a proper job of guidance. In fact, your child may only receive 38 minutes a year (national average) from a high school guidance counselor on college planning. Hmmm…is this enough time to help plan a student's next four years – excuse me, it's *five years* for nearly 70% of the seniors graduating this year. Ever wonder why that is?

If you think 38 minutes will do it, I'm out of business, and please don't bother to send this book to anyone you know who's looking to hire someone like me to actually coach their kid through the process.

Here's the other unspoken problem most guidance counselors never mention: they have their favorite colleges because they've developed a relationship with someone at each of those schools. And they leverage those relationships so the student can get into those colleges. Nothing wrong with that, you say. But think about this: that relationship blurs the objectivity of the counselor who knows she or he will look good if the student is admitted to a "leveraged" college. But where does the "right-fit" come in? Could a counselor's ego or perhaps job security enter this picture?

Trust the student's results. I have each of my students take the Myers-Briggs and Strong assessments. Once they have the results, it's fairly easy to interpret them. Both assessments provide a direction for the student to follow, not an exact occupation. For example, the results may indicate that the student has a strong liking for financial management. That could easily mean that the student ought to look in the direction of majoring in some area that has something to do with – yes! – finances! That would rule out engineering (dad's major) and literature (mom's major). All that needs to be done now is a search for those colleges that have – yes! – majors in the area of finance.

Of course, other factors will come into play on the final selection of a college, such as size and geography. Reputation will be a parent's typical concern, but it isn't the student's so much. Get your heads together and trust your student's instincts on the final decision *after you have visited* your child's top five choices.

The most expensive year is the fifth year: another year of tuition and board, plus a year without being in the work force earning an income. You can avoid this mistake by taking the right steps and an open mind. College for your daughter and son isn't your college anymore. And 38 minutes is a silent catastrophe waiting to happen.

The Ultimate Admission Strategy
And The Easiest

What are the two ideal characteristics every college is looking for in a college applicant? Evidence of leadership - an obsession with colleges - and a passion for something. Perhaps less than 1% of applicants show leadership experience, which means colleges will default to the passion template.

And they don't care what your student is passionate about, just as long as the student is passionate about something. In other words, colleges will just assume your student has no leadership skills.

In this chapter I'm going to illustrate how your student can be part of that 1% and still be considered by classmates and teachers as disengaged from school activities and possibly be considered a dead-head by many. (Gee. I think this describes me when I was in high school....)

What I'm writing about is so easy that mentioning it to a student will either challenge him or her, or give 'em an excuse to do nothing and still appear as a leader. "How can this be?" you ask. Have I been smokin' some Colorado green?

Write a blog. And what's a blog? It's a personal website or web page on which an individual records opinions, links to other sites, etc. on a regular basis.

Okay. Maybe your student isn't a writer, and I'll address that issue in a moment. If s/he likes to write, have the student write a monthly or weekly essay on her passion (which would be ideal). Or on any subject. It doesn't matter.

What does writing a blog signal to the colleges? Remember, you are trying to get your student admitted to a college, which means you have to play this blog thing to the hilt. You're not interested in showing how you can solve the world's problems, but you can observe the world around you by commenting on it in any manner you wish.

One of my coaching students likes to go to the movies. He makes his blog a movie review. One of my former students used her blog to write about - tah-dah! - things around her. Just two examples of what students can do in the privacy of their own homes, undistracted by commitments to after-school activities they hate, or to which they have no commitment, and in which they are leading no one.

But blogs do something unusual. They force the student to think. Colleges like thinkers. Actually they LOVE thinkers. In fact, thinkers are given priority in the admissions office. Why?

Ever wonder why colleges require a college application essay? Partly to see how well students can think for themselves. But here's the subliminal signal that is sent to admission people, something they dream about in an applicant: LEADERSHIP!

How? Since I am the only college planning consultant in the country who's written a highly-praised and reviewed book on leadership, I can tell you that leadership shows up in multiple forms. But since my purpose here is not to review my book, I will simply say that blog writers are thought-leaders - they influence their readers to respond to their thoughts. Plus, blog writers have initiative to do something on their own without any encouragement from others.

Bloggers think independently (Ah! Colleges LOVE *independent* thinkers!). They lead not in front of their classmates with a baseball bat or a soccer ball, but with a keyboard and some fresh ideas. Is that way cool or what?!

Okay. How 'bout the student who doesn't like to write? Here's what your student can do to demonstrate leadership at his or her high school and NEVER write a single word of a blog: start a bloggers group. That automatically makes your student the president of the group.

Note To Student: Spread the word through your teachers that you're looking for students to write only one article for the entire school year. Assign each student to a specific month when they must submit their article (you can have more students and articles if you want). Give them their assignment, which is to write about anything their heart desires. Just once in the school year. Collect the essay from each student by email and put it in the monthly blog. Done. Hardly any work. Maybe 5 minutes a month on a keyboard.

What has this non-writer signaled to the colleges with a resume entry of being president of a writer's club of which s/he was the actual founder?

1. You have initiative (leadership!);
2. You know how to designate (leadership!); and
3. You're the president of the club (leadership!).

Get it? Very little work and no writing. Incredible. Did this student do anything dishonest? No. Underhanded? No. To use a military metaphor, does a general go into actual combat? Does he fire a single bullet? No, but does he get the credit for giving the orders that get the job done? Absolutely.

My approach is honest, deliberate, and focused on one result: standing out in the admissions office. And every college's dream of discovering a leader is fulfilled.

So if you love to write AND you start a bloggers club, you are massively golden in the eyes of every admissions office in the country. And you're doing it because you enjoy it. If you never write a word and you did what I mentioned above, you will have an advantage in the admissions office unlike all the other students who participate in the same usual activities where they are neither presidents nor captains.

For extracurricular activities, concentrate on quality, not quantity, on the unique instead of the standard. The uniqueness of a blogger or being the founder of a writer's club will give your student a profile in every admissions office that colleges dream about.

College Acceptance Rates
Are They Believable?

College acceptance rates are higher, but enrollment rates are getting lower, making the chances of getting into college a whole lot easier. But is this good news for parents and students?

Reuters, the news agency, has an article whose headline indicates that college rejection rates are simply a myth. There is truth in the fact that acceptance rates appear to be encouraging for applicants; note I underscored the word "appear." And we all know that appearances can be deceiving, which makes a documented fact a weak fact - one that cannot be taken seriously.

Let's examine each of the article's points regarding the "myth":

1. The article suggests that over 75% of students who apply to college are accepted. Does it mean that a parent has little reason to be concerned about their little Johnny being accepted to where he applies? By contrast he has a 25% chance of being rejected by those same schools. Sure the odds are in the student's favor, which suggests that both the student and the parent have nothing to worry about. Right?

Let's apply these odds to a medical template. If you were diagnosed with cancer and your doctor said there was a 75% success rate of your cancer evaporating if you had no treatment of any kind, what would your reaction be? I thought so: you'd conclude the doctor was engaging in medical malpractice and you'd seek the best medical advice you could find to increase from 75% to 100%. If a college admissions consultant applied this analogy to your chances of getting into college - and a right-fit college - what would you conclude? Professional malpractice?

2. The article fails to mention the drop-out rates of students who are accepted, which makes you think that the student went to the wrong college. Why? Because they actually didn't qualify academically (28%), but the college accepted Johnny anyway, or the parents simply realized later that a college's long-term commitment (4-6 years) is not affordable (38%).

Conclusion? The parents didn't have a clue of what a real college-fit meant, and they didn't determine well enough in advance if college was genuinely affordable. A no-nonsense hard-bitten college admissions consultant, who could have raised all the red flags in advance and made the proper recommendations, wasn't even considered as a factor in the family's research of colleges.

3. The article mentions that 76% of admission directors are "concerned" about achieving their college enrollment goals. All the more reason to apply anywhere and just, well, wing it. Right? Incredibly in the same paragraph of the article, these same admission directors said that one out of three were offering bigger discounts (read: scholarships and grants) to attract more students.

Okay, so by contrast that means that **two out of three** admission directors are NOT offering more scholarship money to attract more students. Does that mean that MOST admission directors are not so concerned after all? Looks like it to me. And should a parent be worried that the odds of getting more financial aid are against them? Sure looks that way. (Please be patient - I'll return your call.)

In another article that polled college admission directors (read: the Horse's Mouth Society), "61% of private [colleges] and 50% public [colleges] were looking to recruit more international students; and, 65% of private, and 53% of public schools mentioned increasing the recruitment of out-of-state students."

In other words, being admitted to a private or public college as an ordinary American or in-state student is going to get harder.

Here's my crass, shameless, but very helpful suggestion: For real help call me at 1-508-520-6642; I'll pick up the phone or I'll return your call later).

Such articles from news agencies like Reuters are misleading, and when I wanted to add this article to their comments section, which had "no comments" so far, a notice came up on the screen that discussion of this topic was now "CLOSED."

Guidance Counselors
And The Damage They Can Do

Colleges will deny a student's application for admission because the student's guidance counselor failed to send in the paperwork by the college's deadline.

Parents will be scared to know that the ratio of guidance counselors-to-students in America is 470-to-1 (MA 432-to1; CA 1000-1), which means their child's paperwork can easily fall through the cracks at even the best high schools.

What is outrageous is the fact - and parents don't know this - high school guidance counselors, who must get a master's degree to get their jobs, are **never required** to take a single course in college planning. So parents are under the huge misimpression that their child is getting professional college guidance.

A 2010 study from the Bill and Melinda Gates Foundation found that each student gets a total of 38 minutes a year with a counselor to discuss "college." You and I would spend hours planning a vacation, which would cost me 1/50th of the cost of college.

Of course, there are exceptions to every rule. According to the Gates Report, 33% of high school grads said their guidance counselor did a great job on advising about college (read: 67% said their counselor did a "fair or poor job.")

Here are the 3 emails every parent should send to their child's guidance counselor that can prevent the heartbreak of your child's application being refused consideration outright.

First Email: Send 20 Days Before The College's Deadline

> My child's college application to (name of college) is due
> on (date), and I would appreciate your submitting the
> required paperwork not later than 10 days from today.
> I will email you a reminder of this request in 5 days.
> Thank you.

Parent's name (for full name of child

Second Email: Send 5 Days Later

My child's application to (name of college) is due on (date), and I would appreciate your submitting the required paperwork not later than 5 days from today. I will email you in 5 days requesting that you verify your submission of the paperwork.

Thank you.

Parent's name (for full name of child)

Third Email: Send 5 Days Later

By the end of your school day today, I am expecting verification from you by email that you have submitted my child's paperwork to the college. I will also email and call the college in 5 days to verify that you have indeed submitted the required paperwork.

Thank you for your cooperation in this most important matter.

Parent's Name (for full name of child)

The great irony is that guidance counselors are not really at fault. It's the graduate school system that churns out these grads without requiring them to take a single course in college planning. Not one. Only one college in America, Long Island University, requires one course in college financing to receive a masters degree in counseling. In effect, your plumber is equally qualified to be your child's guidance counselor - neither one has any training in college planning. It's scandalous, and I would guess this is the first time you've read this.

The Math Of Admission
Where To Get Accepted

Know exactly where to apply by finding out your chances of admission. But to save time, go to the end of this chapter now.

Why do Harvard and Yale reject over 90% of the best and brightest applicants? Why is any multi-talented and academically-gifted student turned down by an *elite* college or university? There's sameness, where mostly all the applicants have the same ideal GPAs and test scores, and then there's a mismatch. Unless your student meets a predetermined profile of what the college is looking for in their next freshman class, your kid is toast.

I found a company that has the ability to predict a top student's chances for admission to any one of the 150 best undergraduate colleges, and they do it with a 98.2% accuracy rate that comes with a money-back guarantee. After speaking with the enterprising co-founder of the company who attended Princeton University and later received his MBA from Dartmouth's Tuck School of Business, I was impressed enough to suggest the company's services to my clients. When asked what's behind his company's accuracy rate, his reply:

"Our experts have developed unique statistical algorithms for each college that compare a student's background and achievements to the college's numerous admissions criteria including standardized test scores, extracurricular activities, academic record, background and more."

The company stays in constant contact with admissions departments of the most selective schools to get each of their criteria for selection for the next school year. For example, freshmen at one university in 2015 were given preference based on their race, residency, legacy status, athletic prowess and parent-donor status. This is why valedictorians were rejected - they simply didn't meet this school's particular criteria for *that* year.

Getting the best grades and the best test scores are the required start in the right direction, but as I've stated all through this book, there's a lot more that goes into the decision to admit your child, even if you don't like what you've discovered in the section, **The Cost Of Diversity**. On the positive side, your student's achievements and background could very well match better schools that you haven't even considered.

Now you can choose and predict which colleges your high-achieving student has a chance of attending. Statistical data and quantitative analysis are used to accurately match your student to the colleges to which they *should* or should *not* apply, and as an added benefit, it'll save you the expense and time of applying and visiting colleges that won't match. Guess work, parent and student emotions, guidance counselor bias, and your hairdresser's advice are all replaced by an objective template.

To discover where your top student has the best chance of getting into the most selective colleges, go to this website: www.go4college.com

BIG FAT CAUTION: According to a Gallup poll in 2013, American business leaders were asked; "Does where you attend college determine future success?" Ready for this? Ninety-one percent (91%) said "No."

What You Absolutely Must Do Now...

Student: To Get Into The Right-Fit College...

1. Get a study *attitude* by repeating this statement: "I succeed because I love learning." Say it to yourself every chance you get. Post it so you can see it often. Your level of success will depend on the *intensity* of your *belief* in what you're repeating. Read the last sentence again. Start your winning attitude now. And don't stop.

2. Get a study *habit* by studying in 20-minute segments, followed by a 5-minute break. After 20 minutes, stand up and move around. Go back for another 20 minutes and continue the pattern until you have *mastered,* or completed your assignment. During the breaks, enjoy an activity, or get some fresh air. Breaking up your time also avoids getting bored. This pattern will get you better grades. If you repeat what I suggested enough times and commit yourself to this pattern, better grades are in your future. Keep your attitude positive, and avoid negative people.

3. Go to section, *If Your Child Is A High School Junior...,* and follow the directions detailed in the first paragraph.

4. Go to www.dosomething.org. Find just ONE thing you'd love to do, and continue doing this ONE thing all through high school; this website will help you find what kind of community project fits you. When colleges see that you have a passion for *something*, and you get good grades, they'll practically beg you to attend their school. They do it by giving you scholarships and grant money! How cool is that? By having a good study *attitude* and a study *habit*, you'll succeed!

Parent: To Pay For College

1. Encourage your student with what's on the previous page. (Note that I made this # 1)

2. Read and review this book thoroughly.

3. Look at your finances. If you have none to speak of - no stocks, bonds, mutual funds, CDs, gold, jewelry, retirement funds, mattress

money, and piggy banks - you may qualify for lots of financial aid. But you need to know how to maximize your eligibility.

4. If you have assets (don't count money that's already in your retirement), you need to reposition them now. Not next month, but now. Act with a sense of urgency. Most people mistakenly call me the last minute. But if your student is already in high school - *regardless of grade* - you need to take action now.

5. On how to get started, call me for a free chat: 1-508-520-6642.

Parental Tough Love
A Gift To Your Child

You watched the story on TV: An 18-year-old New Jersey student took her parents to court for college expenses and alleged abuse. The judge was smart enough to throw the case out of his court. And it left us wondering what the world was coming to. Guess what? Millions of parents each year are already doing what their teens want them to do: send money weekly while at college; or, parents think they must send spending money so their little cherubs can enjoy the same college experience they had.

Most parents come up with some sort of budget and allocate it on a weekly basis. Yep...it's their conscience in the form of an 18-year-old dictating to the parents what their weekly expense commitment is going to be each year.

That's a disaster in the making. It's called money-dependency and an unintended invitation to move back into the house after graduation. Is their a viable alternative? Tough love parenting in the oh-so-gentle way my wife and I did it.

Tell your children that you will not send one dime while they are in college. Start telling them this when they are in grade school so they get used to this "drip, drip, drip" effect of convincing them that money is never coming their way unless they earn it. Tell them that what they spend while at college will come from only one source: their jobs during the preceding summers or jobs on or off campus during the school year.

I told my two sons that I will force them to get these jobs because I won't send money, that they will be forced to get a job to earn as much spending money as they want.

What will result? What did result? There are two wonderful scenarios at work here:

1. Your child will never learn this from a college economics professor, that is, "you will teach yourself how to budget your money, how to economize, how to avoid frivolous expenses, and how to respect

something as elemental and emotional as the issue of money. You will learn how to be responsible with money."

2. Your child will not have to voice the same complaint that is universal with all recent college grads: "I didn't get a job because I didn't have any experience. How the hell do I get experience if I don't have a job?" In a resume created upon graduation from college, my sons put in this little statement and marked it with a bright yellow highlighter: "Four years on money-management experience." Employers asked what the statement meant. After my sons gave their explanation, the interviewers were so impressed with their work ethic that both sons were offered jobs after *every* interview.

With two sons in college for four years, which is eight years of paying for college, my wife and I figured we saved - in today's dollars - somewhere around $30,000. And in today's dollars, that's nearly two full years of tuition, board and room at an in-state college.

My sons have never asked me for a penny because they do not know what money-dependency means, and today they work at good-paying jobs; their employers enjoy the benefit of witnessing their work ethic in action everyday.

My sons's appreciation for money and independence were gifts my wife and I gave them at no cost to us. The experience was a win-win.

Acknowledgements

Thanks to Dr. George R. Boggs, President and CEO of the American Association of Community Colleges, I was able to make some slight but necessary adjustments to the section, *Best Kept Secret*.

Dan Maga, who owns his own financial planning firm near Chicago, has been very informative regarding the financial issues that are found in this book, and he's an impressive advisor.

Then there's the energetic professor, Ron Caruthers of Carlsbad, California, who makes me wish I were back in college just to have him as a teacher. Ron's enthusiasm is contagious, and financial aid experts, let alone his own customers, are inspired every time he speaks about his favorite subject.

Curtis Smith, a Chartered Financial Consultant from Charlestown, RI, has been a mentor and an inspiration over the years on how to best satisfy the financial needs of my clients. His "the client comes first" philosophy demonstrates an integrity and character that makes me proud of our association.

Other financial experts who provided insight into my chapters on Income and Assets were Jeffrey Shank and John Hollosy.

Finally, my wife, Ann Marie, was understanding of my efforts to help "my students," as I like to call them, and remained most supportive of seeing this book through to its completion.

Article Sources

Warning

Alan M. Dershowitz's interview on the Hugh Hewitt radio show, transcript published on www.hughhewitt.com, 2/25/06; *Poison Ivy*, The Economist, 9/23/06; "Families are stretching even more to attend a public four-year college...spending 21 percent of their income. Private colleges are the most expensive, requiring that families spend a stunning 33 percent of their income." *Paying for College: The Rising Cost of Higher Education*, MassINC study by B. T. Long, Dana Ansel and Greg Leiserson, 4/06; "Over half of students graduating from four-year colleges in the U. S. lack the literacy to deal with such 'real life' tasks as understanding newspaper editorials, comparing credit card offers, or summarizing the results of a survey,"..."Nor do they have the math skills needed to balance their checkbooks, according to a new study by the Pew Charitable Trusts." *Cash $trapped Colleges*, quoting David Schaefer of Holy Cross College, The Conservative Voice, Malcolm A. Kline, 4/30/06; The Ivy League mindset may be summarized by this question from Richard Baehr, The American Thinker blog, *The College Rejection Bonanza*, 4/7/06: "So why are the elite schools able to take so much pleasure in delivering unprecedented quantities of bad news?" He offers six answers to the question; for insight into what the Ivies think of themselves, the president of Brown welcomed the new freshman class: "You are the smartest, the cutest, the savviest, most dynamic, extraordinary -- I could go on and on." Wall Street Journal, 5/1/06; in his LA Times op-ed piece (4/13/06), *Higher Education: The Status Game,* the president of Colby College admits: "Our students and their parents want to hear--and are told--that they are several cuts above the pack." Apparently, a function of our elitist schools is to plant early the seeds of narcissism and self-absorption; an honest assessment of tuition increases comes from a non-elitist college president, Daniel S. Cheever, Jr., *Is College Worth the Money?* Boston Globe, 6/3/05: "What never seems to end for students and parents, however, is understandable anxiety over paying for college. The relentless rise in the costs of higher education alarms payers and the public." With some urgency, he cautions fellow academics: "College officials must take this issue more seriously." But will they? With brazen sarcasm, the president of Johns Hopkins University made no effort to assuage parental concerns about costs: "Why not reconfigure the Homewood campus into a college for seniors — those over 65 who want to go back and experience the college life perhaps they never had? The golden years group will not be as concerned about tuition costs." *Expensive Tuition? Take Some Tips from Corporate America - Relocate to Cozumel,* William R. Brody, Baltimore Business Journal, 2/27/04; for a scathing critique of college professors, see Al Doyle's *The Biggest Con Game in America,* lewrockwell.com, 5/31/05; here's how a smug and elitist college official responds to counselors who help students get into college and parents save money: "The counseling isn't worth it...Nauseous doesn't begin to describe my reaction...it's a vile, vulgar, cynical rip-off..." *College-Admissions Boot Camp for $10,000 Draws Educators' Ire,* Brian Sullivan and Liz Willen, Bloomberg.com, 5/20/05; and here's how one Smith College professor judges many of his own colleagues: "... it's incredible to me how many erstwhile scholars routinely violate one of the sacred precepts of academia: collegiality. They behave as if they are a sun about which all others rotate like space debris. They prattle on about their own research as if they were uncrowned princes holding court, seldom shutting up long enough to ask others about their work, or bothering to disguise their disinterest when the topic strays from any subject other than themselves." *How To Sabotage Your Career,* 11/7/06 Rob Weir, InsideHigherEd.com

Economics101

Quote from the admissions director of Purdue Univ, US News & World Report, 8/29/05, p 66.

2 DirtySecrets

"To help make a Fairfield University education more affordable, administrators there are raising tuition and room and board next year by close to 6 percent. No, really...a freshman biology major at Fairfield U., questions the logic." *Fairfield U., SHU more costly*, L.C. Lambeck, Connecticut Post Online, 5/2/05; *College president shows he's out of touch*, Mike Woods, postcrescent.com, 5/8/2008, with this telling statement: "I know you've often heard college presidents are frauds, hypocrites, and, well, morons. And you wonder how can this be."; CNN Money, Sarah Max, 5/3/05; Associated Press: *Univ of Washington Considers High Tuition-High Aid Model*, 9/2/05; Alan Finder, *Aid Lets Smaller Colleges Ask, "Why Pay for Ivy League Retail?"* NY Times, 1/1/06; 2006 NACUBO Endowment Study, see www.nacubo.org/pressroom; *US bid to keep tabs on tuition irks colleges*, Boston Globe, 7/16/05: "'When the federal government is spending tens of billions of dollars on higher education, and we're asking for a little accountability, then there's no reason why these schools can't provide us with information about why their tuition and fees are increasing,' said...a spokesman for Representative Buck McKeon...." "Despite what they see as statistical shortcomings, some [college] administrators do fear that an unfavorable index could hurt a college's image in a competitive market." Translation: exposing a college's value-for-money-spent formula could prove damaging; a former Brown University admissions director "found the 'quintessential diamond in the rough' -- a black student who had previously not considered a school like Brown." *Building Diversity*, Daily Pennsylvanian, Deena Greenberg, 4/11/06; the hypocrisy of elite colleges may be tied to the QuestBridge College Match program, which in 2005 matched only *46 low-income students* in the nation with full 4-year scholarships to some of the nation's best colleges. See www.questbridge.org; it's been noted that Bronx Community College has 7,200 black and Hispanic students, which is "about as many black and Hispanic undergraduates as there are in the eight Ivy League universities combined." InsiderHigherEd.com, *Anxiety, Values and Undergrad Education*, 4/16/2007; note the title of this Ivy League newspaper article, *Colleges vie for low-income students*, and its self-serving conclusion: "From kindergarten on, [lower-income students] are less likely to attend good schools. Their parents are less likely to have a college education that might help them chart a path to the Ivy League. They do not have access to the SAT coaching, the summer programs or the advising services that have all become staples of the college search for wealthy families." Yale Daily News, 4/27/06; "Some specialists also blame private universities' practice of using a chunk of limited financial aid funds for merit scholarships so they can enroll the most attractive students regardless of whether those students need help. That leaves less money for those who simply need the aid." Boston Globe, 5/1/06; "Church officials said that multiple real estate developers expressed interest in the land, but that Boston College won the bidding because, with its $1.15 billion endowment, the Jesuit university is able to pay cash up front..." *Diocesan headquarters sold to BC*, Boston Globe, 4/21/04; a BC spokesman was asked about the 2006 tuition increase: "Excellence is an expensive proposition," and added that "... spiraling energy costs, and the increasing cost of health insurance for BC employees were also reasons for the increase." The Heights, 4/6/06; when its president, Rev. William Leahy, was asked if BC would ever stop raising tuition, his response was not a sympathy plea to paying parents: "A billion dollars is a great amount of money, but it by no means eliminates all the pressure." Associated Press, Justin Pope, 5/22/05; a college whose endowment (cash stash) exceeds $650,000,000 responded to an aid request from a high-achieving student from a struggling family: "We have reviewed your letter requesting additional financial aid from Northeastern University. We acknowledge that your circumstances are compelling; however, we feel your current award reflects our best effort to reduce your financial burden." Copy of response is in this author's possession; in the most dramatic display of illogical behavior, not uncommon on American college campuses, Yale University admitted a former official of the brutal Taliban regime and defender of the torture of women, but rejected 19,000 innocent applicants in 2006, *Yale Undergrads: The Best, The Brightest, The Taliban?* Janet McMonagle, www.families.com, 5/6/06; in his book, *The Price of Admission*, author Dan Golden says the elite colleges are "mastering the art of perpetuating themselves" by giving admissions preference to wealthy applicants over new immigrants and Asian-Americans. No surprise; "According to a 2006 Education Sector report, the amount of 'merit' aid awarded to students increased fivefold from 1994 to 2000, more than four times the rate of increase for need-based aid. In 2002, the federal Advisory Committee on Student Financial Assistance concluded that low-income students at private four-year colleges have $6,200 of unmet need each year, more than twice the average unmet need of high-income students. Over a dozen state universities have also shifted resources to give more money to high-scoring students, regardless of financial need, according to a 2002 Civil Rights Project report." *Charting a fairer path to college*, Nina M. Marks, courier-journal.com, 5/13/2007; the statistic regarding the dropout rate of first-generation students comes from this article; see *Shopping for a good college should be made easier*: "U.S. Education Secretary Margaret Spellings has made an intriguing proposal - grade colleges and universities on their ability to turn out productive and competent graduates." Fosters.com, 6/17/2007.

AskToughQuestions

WashingtonSquareNews, 4/13/05; Hubert Herry's article in the NY Times, 4/17/05; *Prospies weigh College's cost in decision*, "...gifted middle-class students must weigh whether attending a top-tier college like Dartmouth is worth the loans their parents will be taking out for that name brand to adorn their sweatshirts and eventually their college diplomas." Dartmouth Online, 4/22/05; Boston Globe, *College: Beyond the Pricetag*, 8/8/05; Dr. Ron Melcher's post on www.carnegiefoundation.org, 5/27/05, 2:22:39 pm; *The College Rejection Bonanza*, Richard Baehr, The American Thinker, 4/7/06; *Saying 'No Thanks' to the Ivy League*: "Even as the price of attending an elite college approaches $50,000 a year, less-prestigious schools are offering more merit aid, making the cost differences starker." Robert Tomsho, Wall Street Journal, 4/24/06; *Estimating the Pay-Off to Attending a More Selective College: An Application of Selection on Observables and Unobservables*, Dale, Stacy Berg and Alan B. Krueger, National Bureau of Economic Research, Inc., 1999; other researchers came to the opposite conclusion, finding that "even after controlling for selection effects, there is strong evidence of significant economic return to attending an elite private institution." See Brewer, Dominic J., Eric R. Eide and Ronald G. Ehrenberg, *Does It Pay To Attend An Elite Private College? A Cross-Cohort Evidence On The Effects Of College Type On Earnings*, Journal of Human Resources, 1999, vol 34, pp 104-123. This is another way academics demonstrate that for every action there's an equal and opposite reaction. Reality: we all deal with the hand we've been dealt with no regrets that we didn't attend an Ivy League school; the National Center for Education Statistics "shows that of the 1,314,506 faculty members at colleges that award federal financial aid in fall 2005, 624,753, or 47.5 percent, were in part-time positions...an increase in number and proportion from 2003, the last full survey of institutions, when 543,137 of the 1,173,556 professors (or 46.3 percent) at degree-granting institutions were part timers." Insidehighered.com, 3/28/07.

The 4-Letter Word Quote from The Bowdoin Orient online, 9/16/05; the quote referring to the new décor of a financial aid office, Boston Globe, 3/20/05; for an equally boneheaded remark from another elitist college in Maine: "But [the dean] recognizes the $55 application fee is an obstacle and a financial burden for some students,..." Let's see if you get this: you're applying to a college whose cost of attendance exceeds $45,000 a year, and a dean says prospective students regard $55 as "an obstacle and a financial burden." Either he's smoking something odd, or you're the type who can't justify buying the house of your dreams because you find the cost of the doorbell "an obstacle and a burden."*Colby College Waives*

Application Fee for Maine Students, press release 8/18/05.

The Cost Of Diversity The US Supreme Court ruled in 2003 that race can be used as a factor in college admissions (Grutter v. Bollinger through compliance with Regents of Univ. of CA v. Bakke); incredibly, the National Association for College Admission Counseling (NACAC), a nationwide group of more than 9,800 high school counselors, independent counselors, college admissions and financial aid officers, endorses a congressional plan to give illegals (this group calls them "undocumented") equal access to the American educational system: "As counselors and admission officers dedicated to improving college access nationwide, we hope that Congress will continue to act positively on behalf of these students in order to ensure they have the opportunity to pursue higher education and to make a strong contribution to our country." *Nation's College Admission Counselors Applaud Lofgren Hearing on Undocumented Students,* newswireascribe.org, 5/18/2007; to participate in the educational system "in the name of diversity, the academic elites have encouraged immigrants to maintain their birth-country cultures and to adopt a stance of separatism and pugnacious victimization." *Sentiment Against Illegals Is Powerful & Growing,* John Leo, RealClearPolitics website, 5/7/06; *Parent Trap,* David Epstein www.insidehighered.com, 7/6/05; *No More Cheating For A Good Cause,* David Gelernter, LA Times, 7/22/05; *College Faculties A Most Liberal Lot,* Howard Kurtz, Washington Post, 3/29/05; *Colorblind Merit has no merit for University of California,* Thomas Lifson, American Thinker blog, 7/15/05; *Why Does College Cost So Much?,* Richard Vedder, Wall Street Journal, 8/23/05; The federal law being broken by 8 states (NY, CA, WA, TX, UT, OK, IL, KS) is Title 8, Chapter 14, Sec. 1623, which states, "an alien who is not lawfully present in the United States shall not be eligible on the basis of residence within a State...for any postsecondary education benefit unless a citizen or national of the United States is eligible for such a benefit." *The Left University: How to Overcome It,* James Piereson, Weekly Standard, 10/03/05; *The College Gender Shift,* Howard and Matthew Greene, Knight Ridder/Tribune News Service, 3/24/04; *A Herd of Academic Minds,* Ed Feulner, Washington Times website, 11/7/05; *Slurring Bush at the New York Times,* Richard Baehr, American Thinker Blog, 5/23/05; *To All The Girls I've Rejected,* Jennifer D. Britz, NY Times, 3/23/06; *Survey reveals pervasive political pressure in the classroom,* American Council of Trustees and Alumni press release, 11/30/04; Thomas Sowell, *College Brainwashing,* RealClearPolitics website, 3/14/06; Oregon State University's "conservative student newspaper, The Liberty, exists on $4,000 a year in private contributions compared to the half a million dollars that the student government spends on a panoply of gay, feminist and environmental groups." *Conservative Student Backlash,* Malcolm A. Kline, The Conservative Voice, 2/17/06; for one school's rationale for discrimination, see Harvard Univ Gazette online (4/6/06): "A significant number of other incoming students will also bring an international perspective..."; "Yale University enrolls a former Taliban official with a 4th grade education into a non-degree program in the name of diversity, while the University of California attempts to discriminate against students educated at Christian high schools. DePaul University repeatedly makes war on the free speech rights of conservative students and faculty. Stanford University and the College of the Holy Cross attempt to silence the powerful independent voices of their respective established alternative newspapers. On the fourth anniversary of 9/11, Canisius College tries to avoid commemorating the victims, while the University of Iowa opts to hold a 'Peacefest', inviting numerous radical groups including socialists and pacifists, instead of honoring the victims of the national tragedy. Diversity run amok, suppression of free speech, and discrimination against Christians, conservatives, and patriots continue to be the norm in American higher education, and the Collegiate Network (CN) has once again chronicled the worst of those abuses in its 9th Annual Campus Outrage Awards." *2006 Campus Outrage Awards,* www.campusmagazine.org, 4/3/06; "It's no secret that American universities, while trumpeting 'diversity,' are among the least diverse places in the Western world." *Intellectual Diversity Unwelcome At American Universities,* Roger Kimball, RealClearPolitics, 12/19/06; Professor Vedder's TV interview in *Why Does College Cost So Much and Is It Worth It?* Fox News, September 2, 2006; the state of Texas has a better idea of diversity: guarantee admission to any state university to students who graduate in the top 10% of their class (Hopwood v. Texas, 1996); *Admission Preferences for Minority Students, Athletes, and Legacies at Elite Universities,* Social Science Quarterly 85 (5), 1422-1446, Thomas J. Espenshade, Chang Y. Chung, Joan L. Walling, 2004; on page 12 of *Religious Beliefs & Behavior of College Faculty,* Vol II, authors Tobin and Weinberg said that 53% of American college professors hold unfavorable feelings toward Evangelican Christians, but only 22% had unfavorable feelings toward Muslims. 2007, Institute for Jewish & Community Research; *College Admission: Tough Times For Girls?* CBS News website, Alex Kingsbury of US News & World Report, posted 10/13/2007.

How & Where To Get Free Money Ball State University's and Stonehill's grant-to-loan ratios, www.collegeboard.com, 5/11/06.

Bad Advice Michael Abernethy, *College education costs rising more and more*, Free Press, Kingston, NC, 8/14/05; Washington Post article by Albert Crenshaw, 8/16/05; *Increase your odds on college aid*, Candace Bahr, www.NCTimes.com, 8/17/05; *Don't hurt yourself when seeking college aid*, R. Shaffer, Boston Herald, 10/9/05; stats on projected costs at state schools from the American Association of State Colleges and Universities, 2004-2005; *Learning the college financial aid system*, A. M. Chaker, Wall Street Journal, 3/28/06.

Admissions101 http://www.educationalconsulting.org

Before The Junior Year From the 2007 New York University website on what the college looks for in an applicant: "In general, we would prefer to see substantial involvement in a few activities rather than superficial involvement in a laundry list of clubs and organizations. We particularly like to see evidence of leadership roles." *To All The Girls I've Rejected*, J. D. Britz, NY Times, 3/23/06; see www.go4college.com on how to minimize rejection - or maximize acceptance - at the top 150 schools; "The extra something—a passion or commitment communicated in a clear voice— is what many admissions counselors at top schools say they are looking for." "I think we're all looking for kids who are committed to something, extracurricularly, intellectually, and hopefully both." Brown University dean's comments in the Wall Street Journal, *Who Got Into College?* 4/13/06; "No extracurricular activity experience can take the place of good grades earned in a college-preparatory curriculum." Duquesne University's Paul Cukanna, *Who Gets In? College Admission Officials Offer Their Advice On College Admissions*, Pittsburg-Post Gazette, 2/15/06; "The successful students have to have shown some passion for science and technology in high school or their personal life," said Jill Perry, a Caltech spokeswoman. "That means creating a computer system for your high school, or taking a tractor apart and putting it back together." *Admission to elite colleges got tougher,* April 4, 2007, Time Argus, 4/7/2207.

Your College Application *Lying and Deception*, Paul Ekman, Memory For Everyday and Emotional Events, Ornstein & Tversky, Lawrence Erlbaum Publishers, NJ, 1997; "Anyone can say that you need to have good grades and good standardized test scores to get into college. That is a given. If you find that you are an average student in terms of GPA and standardized testing performance, I have found that there is one little word that can make the difference between being accepted to a university, being put on the waiting list, and being denied admission: Presentation." "In the age of the online application, following very simple rules can separate your application from those of other students. Make sure that your application is neatly presented." "Just because many online applications are free does not mean that you should be nonchalant about how you fill it out. These tips may sound too simple, but you'd be astounded to see how many students do not follow them." John Carroll University's assistant director of admission, Kevin M. Hatgas, *Who Gets In? College Admission Officials Offer Their Advice On College Admissions*, Pittsburg-Post Gazette, 2/15/06.

How To Apply To College "Students who take this [essay] opportunity to think about who they are, how they function in their world, what is important to them, and the ways in which they impact others not only produce effective essays, but also increase their insight and self-awareness. This thoughtful self-analysis increases the likelihood that the student will make good choices about the college he will attend, and will begin college with an understanding of why the college he selected is a good match for him." *College applications*, Joan H. Bress, Worcester Magazine, 8/10-16/2006; "Interviewers are under strict orders to be charming and warm, no matter what they think of a candidate. The object of an interview, from the college's point of you, is to give you a terrific experience of their school. It's a recruiting tool." Plus, "...they take up too much time gathering largely useless information..." *On Writing the College Application Essay: The Key to Acceptance and the College of your Choice,* Harry Bauld, Quill (HarperResource), 1987, p. 6; "Often the essay is the only piece of the application that is unique to each student." Case Western Univ's senior assistant in admissions, Diane Feckanin's and Temple's Mary Beth Kurilko's quotes in *Who Gets In? College Admission Officials Offer Their Advice On College Admissions*, Pittsburg-

Post Gazette, 2/15/06; "…the level of advocacy for students and the relationship with admissions counselors played a much larger role" this year. *Who Got Into College?* A.M. Chaker, Wall Street Journal, 4/13/06; *How Admission Decisions Are Made*, www.educationplanner.com, Amer Ed Services, 2006; Dartmouth College's statement on their Peer Evaluation form: "We suggest a candid statement, covering both personal and academic qualities. Specific anecdotes are much more helpful than general observations. We are interested in learning about this student's contributions to school or community, ability to work with others, and his/her interests, special talents and experiences"; *The New Rules of College Admissions*, p. 101: "When a school takes both the Common Application and its own, my advice is to use the Common"; *Ibid*, p. 108: "Setting your child apart in the college admissions process requires the articulation of a single theme that transcends the entire application and is visible in every individual part."

Dumb Stuff On its Peer Evaluation form for the Class of 2011, this is Dartmouth College's full statement: "We would appreciate a statement, *on the reverse side of this form*, based on your knowledge and observation of this candidate. We suggest a candid statement, covering both personal and academic qualities. Specific anecdotes are much more helpful than general observations. We are interested in learning about this student's contributions to school or community, ability to work with others, and his/her interests, special talents, and experiences. Do you have any reservations about his/her application to Dartmouth? We welcome all comments you feel are relevant."; The National Center on Addiction and Substance Abuse at Columbia University, *Wasting the Best and the Brightest: Substance Abuse at America's Colleges and Universities.* "The study also finds that 1.8 million full-time college students (22.9 percent) meet the medical criteria for substance abuse and dependence, two and one half times the 8.5 percent of the general population who meet these same criteria." The study also revealed that 49% (3.8 million) full-time students binge drink or abuse drugs. Binge drinking is defined as 5 drinks in a row for men and 4 drinks in a row for women within a 2-week period; or, getting drunk at least twice a month. See www. consumeraffairs.com, 3/15/2007; for Paul Cukann's remark, see http://www.post-gazette.com/pg/06046/655203.stm; regarding the value of taking the SAT and ACT tests often, "We don't care how many times you take it," said Mrs. Taylor, an admissions counselor for the University of California at Berkeley. She said she doesn't know of any schools that average students' SAT scores after taking the exam for the third time. Bette Johnson, associate director of admissions for MIT, also said that she doesn't know of any schools that penalize students for taking the SAT three times. She suggested that to make sure you check with the colleges to which you are applying. The Naval Academy actually encourages students to take the test two or three times to achieve the highest possible scores. So go ahead and take the exam again for the third time." http://www.supercollege.com/ask.cfm? loc=4&page=3&story=306&topic=16&cart=1

FAFSA FUMBLE Regarding timing of repositioning a student asset, check this statement from a financial aid office in Boston: "If you fill out the FAFSA and hand it in and then reorganize your assets, you haven't shown everything that's in your name. That's fraud." To avoid fraud move the asset *before* filling out the paperwork, ideally before Jan 1 of the year you fill out the FAFSA. *BU Warns Against Some Methods Of Getting Financial Aid*, Daily Free Press.com, 2/6/2007. Repositioning assets is perfectly legal and ethical; the Department of Education "found that most families, from all income levels, had trouble completing the form. Although the Student Financial Aid office within the U.S. Department of Education has made strides in this area, the financial aid process is still a maze and deterrent for many families." *A Framework For Student Retention*, studentretention.org, 5/13/2007.

SAT & ACT "Research shows that the average student who retests increases his or her combined critical reading and mathematics scores by approximately 30 points." www.collegeboard.com; *Another College Drops Standardized Test Requirement for Admissions*, AACRAO Transcript, www.aacrao.org, Heather Zimar, 5/18/05; "The ACT is a competitor test to the SAT. Colleges view the ACT as an equally valid standardized test and ALL colleges accept either test score. The ACT tests a broader range of subject matter than the SAT: while ACT has math and verbal skills similar to those on the SAT, the ACT has trigonometry, a 'Science Reasoning' section testing data interpretation, and occasional questions on logarithms, matrices and imaginary numbers. The ACT's breadth makes it a more difficult test to study for. The exception is students with a weak vocabulary, as vocabulary is extensively tested in the Sentence completion sections of the SAT, sections that do not appear on the ACT." *SAT, PSAT, ACT and SAT IIs - A Primer for Beginners,* www.eisinc.com/release/storiesh/GREENS.013.html; *SAT Optional Colleges On The Rise,* Silver Chips Online, Michelle Caabrese, 1/28/07: "Bates conducted a 20-year study of the academic differences between University students who submitted their scores and who did not. They found that the average college GPA of a submitter is 3.11, while the average college GPA of a non-submitter is 3.06. 'Once they are here at Bates, they do equally well,' explained Belka. The difference in Bates graduation rates between submitters and non-submitters is 0.1 percent."; *Admission Matters,* p. 118: "The questions on the ACT are tied more to what a student has learned in school in grades 7 through 12 than to critical thinking and problem solving in general." "Colleges not only require the SAT, but 'reward you' if you can afford to take the test multiple times and bring up your score,.." *Anxiety, Values and Undergrad Education,* Scott Jaschik, Inside-HigherEd.com, 4/16/2007.

Senior Moment The acceptance letter from Monmouth University in New Jersey is my favorite for its bluntness, if not its dreadful subtlety with the last word in this P.S. of the letter: "Your admission to the university is contingent upon satisfactory completion of current course work. Please make arrangements to have a final transcript sent to the Office of Admission Processing. Please note that Monmouth University reserves the right to revoke admission from accepted students if the course work is not completed *satisfactorily.*" (Italics added)

Getting The Most Aid *College Aid Stratagems,* Forbes.com, Ashlea Ebeling, 3/13/06. Colleges that multiply your income by 1.2% to determine the equity in your home: Amherst, Boston College, Brown, Claremont-McKenna, Columbia, Cornell, Dartmouth, Davidson, Duke, Emory, Georgetown, Grinnell, Haverford, MIT, Middlebury, Northwestern, Pomona, Rice, Swarthmore, University of Chicago, Notre Dame, UPenn, Vanderbilt, Wake Forest, Wellesley, Wesleyan, Williams, and Yale; *Access To College Counseling,* www.nacanet.org, bottom of page 1; "...research has shown that grants are a much better predictor of students' persistence [retention] than loans (Astin, 1982; U.S. General Accounting Office, 1995) ..." *A Framework For Student Retention,* studentretention.org, 5/13/2007; keeping first-year students from dropping out is a cottage industry within academia. There's even a national organization called the National Center for the Study of the Freshman Year Experience, created in 1987 by the Univ of South Carolina; "...only 68.3 percent of all first-year college students returned to the same institution for the second-year in 2005, and that this information is 'remarkably similar to results in previous years.'" *The First Year College Experience: Strategies For Improvement,* Jeffrey M. Kelley, edited 5/1/06 in www.newfoundations.com/OrgTheory.

Pick A College "...students need to weigh the importance of a four-year finish against other priorities. Second majors, internships, activities and outside study may all enrich the experience but may also add to the time spent getting a degree." "Increasingly, college is shifting from a four-course meal to a collection of credits amassed a la carte." "More students earn credit from more than one college, whether they formally transfer or pick up courses at home over the summer." *Different Paths Lead To A Degree,* Kate Holloway, USA TODAY website, 11/9/05; *College Blogs Tell It Like It Is,* Marcella Bombardieri, Boston Globe, 4/16/2007: "The message from student bloggers isn't always pretty, yet college officials say the blogs are worth the risk. High school students can get unvarnished views of any colleges from Facebook, MySpace, or unsanctioned student blogs. They may be more inclined to trust a school they think is willing to show them real campus life, officials say. Plus, the technology gives colleges another tool to help applicants make the best decision, especially if they cannot afford to fly in for an overnight stay."

Scholarship Highjacking Boston U's website: www.bu.edu/finaid, 5/11/06; From the Finaid.org website: "The Federal overaward regulations in 34 CFR

673.5(b) requires colleges to take into account any resources they know about or can anticipate when awarding or disbursing aid. In addition, 34 CFR 673.5(d) requires colleges to reduce the size of the need-based aid package whenever the student receives resources that exceed financial need by more than $300." Here's how the University of Virginia, with an endowment in 2006 of $3,618,000,000 (that's over 3 BILLION!) answers a student's inquiry on their blog about scholarships: "Unfortunately, the [private] scholarship funds usually first replace the grants that you are given in your Award Package. I know, it seems unfair, but it allows our Financial Aid Office to spread the funds to cover all students with need. Congratulations on earning a scholarship!" In other words, "we don't care that you worked hard and earned a well-deserved scholarship, we're taking it away and giving it to someone else who needs it more than you do." This last statement is purely the interpretation of the author and does not necessarily reflect the opinions of the university president, faculty, board of directors, alumni, donors, and, of course, its janitorial staff. http://accessuva.blogspot.com, 6/5/2007.

EarlyEarlyEarlyEarlyEarly *Early Decision: College Experts Forum,* Comments from David Hawsey, www.collegeconfidential.com, 5/11/06; *The Early Admissions Game,* Avery, Fairbanks and Zeckhauser, p. 137.

22 Income Strategies This list is the most relevant. For a list with more narrowly-focused items, see The Princeton Review, Edition 2007.

Asset Strategies *College Aid Stratagems,* Ashlea Ebeling, Forbes.com, 3/13/06; "Retirement funds and pensions are generally not considered assets by both the Federal Methodology and the Institutional Methodology need analysis formulas. You can shelter a considerable portion of your assets by making the maximum contributions to these funds in the years *before* the base year. Likewise, tax-deferred annuities and life insurance policies (e.g., single-premium, universal and whole life insurance policies) are not considered assets by the need analysis system." www.finaid.org/fafsa/maximize, section on Assets, # 7; "Funds deposited in modified endowment contracts aren't counted...in aid calculations."

Parental assets lower college aid, John F. Wasik, Bloomberg News Service, 4/2/2007. Author Wasik then suggests that these plans are subject to taxes and penalties before age 59 ½. That's true for nearly all MECs, except for the one that I recommend to my clients; "When you buy a house, you get to deduct points paid to get your mortgage in one fell swoop. When you refinance a mortgage, though, you have to deduct the points over the life of the loan. That means 1/30th a year if it's a 30 year mortgage -- that's $33 a year for each $1,000 of points you paid. Not much, maybe, but don't throw it away. And, in the year you pay off the loan -- because you sell the house or refinance again -- you may get to deduct all as-yet-undeducted points. You do unless you refinance with the same lender. In that case, you add points on the latest deal to the leftovers from the previous refinancing and deduct the expense ratably over the life of the new loan." *The 13 Most Overlooked Tax Deductions,* Kevin McCormally, Kiplinger.com, 1/31/2007.

529s, UTMAs & UGMAs You won't know how each school will structure your financial aid package until after they see *your* 529. Then it's time to cross your fingers, arms, legs, and eyeballs. Is this any way to purchase a college-aid plan, filled with mystery, at the mercy of *each college's own policy* toward 529s, loss of control over how your money is invested, multiple fees, and subject to regulatory crackdowns on the marketing practices of brokers? "They're top-class investments. But they could fail you miserably...funding Coverdells and 529s could be a huge mistake. Confused? Blame it on the bizarre world of college financial aid." *It Pays to Study College-Savings Plans,* Jonathan Clements, Wall Street Journal, 5/10/04; *Paying For College,* Princeton Review, 2005 Edition, p. 32; *The real deal on college savings,* Reuters, posted online, 12/16/05; www.savingforcollege.com; "Ameriprise Financial Inc. has agreed to pay fines after regulators alleged inadequate disclosure to clients, *and other firms have also reached settlements* (Italics added). The Municipal Securities Rulemaking Board, which regulates broker sales of 529 plans, recently agreed to strengthen disclosure and other rules for marketers of the plans." *529 Plans Lose Their Luster,* A.M. Chaker, College Journal website, Wall Street Journal, 3/6/06; "In distributing their own aid, however, colleges often look at all 529 plans that name the student as beneficiary.

So even if the strategy works for the federal-aid calculation, it won't necessarily work for the institution." *Ready For Financial Aid?* A.M. Chaker, article appearing in the Charlotte Observer online, 12/31/06; See provision S. 9132 of the Higher Education Reconciliation Act of 2005 which states, **"The net value of small businesses with not more than 100 full-time equivalent employees is excluded from the definition of 'assets'";** "So 529 plans opened by grandparents go uncounted in the *federal* calculus." A.M. Chaker, *Answering readers' questions about financial aid,* http://www.post-gazette.com/pg/06352/747077-298.stm; "But nobody will tell you it's easy to get started. The main reason? There are so many 529 plans out there! Almost every state offers at least one, and each has its own slightly different rules and requirements. Choosing among them has unfortunately become a confusing and cumbersome affair." *The Ins and Outs of 529 Plans,* Harold Simansky, collegetollkit.com; "Some states offer 529 plans with fees that are indefensibly high. That in itself may not be so alarming. Just as there are good mutual funds and bad funds, there are good 529 plans and bad plans. But so far folks do not seem to be able to discern between the two, because they're being herded into high-cost plans that have little tax benefit." http://www.bankrate.com/bosre/news/BoomerBucks, *Flaws Showing In 529 Plans For College Savings,* Barbara Whelehan, 10/16/2006.

Start A Business During College Years MSN's Jeff Schnepper, money-central.msn.com/content/taxes; and www.chrisbirdseminars.com

Best Kept Secret US News & World Report, 8/29/05, p. 64; *How to cut college costs,* A. M. Chaker, Wall Street Journal, 8/15/2005. Kay M. MCClenney, Director, Community College Survey of Student Engagement, Community College Leadership Program, Univ. of Texas at Austin and her interview on website www.decliningbydegrees.org. Her comments describe the similarities of community colleges with small elite liberal arts colleges; Dr. Gamble's remarks on www.carnegiefoundation.org, posted 5/26/05; the American Association of Community College's website: "Community college students learn in relatively small classes from instructors whose primary responsibility is teaching, not research, and average student-teacher contact time is higher at community colleges than at other higher education institutions." This reads like a description of a small 4-year private college in the 1960s. Are community colleges already "back to the future?" "Amy" posted an insightful statement on her experience with her community college (CC), 5/5/06, on www.insidehighered.com.

After The Award Letter *A helpful family guide to college financing,* Terry Savage, Chicago Sun Times, 5/2/05; alarmingly, the Princeton Review advises, "If you can comfortably afford the amount the school says you must pay, then there is little chance that the school is going to sweeten the deal – it must be pretty good already." This would suggest that schools are generous. I appeal all awards with one attitude, "It's not enough."

If Your Aid Isn't Enough Colleges that won't allow you to go to a private lender for your parent PLUS or Stafford loans are part of this group: "The National Direct Student Loan Coalition (NDSLC) is an alliance of schools participating in the Federal Direct Student Loan Program. We are the only organization solely devoted to representing the interests and concerns of direct lending institutions: 1,100 colleges and universities around the country." This organization's website cites the positive testimonials from 23 colleges, but none mention the rate each has achieved for its students.

US News & World Report Gerhard Casper, president of Stanford University: "...much of these rankings – particularly their specious formulas and spurious precision – is utterly misleading." *Admission Matters,* Sally P. Springer and Marion R. Franck. Jossey-Bass, A Wiley Imprint, 2005, p. 10; "Most numbers used in constructing scores for such rankings can be manipulated and are manipulated," Malcolm Getz, an associate professor of economics at Vanderbilt University and author of the book *Investing in College: A Guide for the Perplexed,* said." *Colleges Knock 'U.S. News,'* www.tennessean.com, Ralph Loos, 3/25/07; "The importance of going to a college with a high reputation has remained virtually unchanged since 1983, according to responses, but rankings have factored in as increasingly important in making that determination. Still, only 16.4 percent of [student] respondents found rankings to be very important in their overall decision." *The American Freshman: Forty-Year Trends 1966–2006,* UCLA's Cooperative Institutional Research Program Freshmen Survey, 2007; here's how one economics writer describes the US News college edition: "...this *destructive* (italics added) publication..." *Getting Past Prestige Names When Searching For A College,* signonsandiego.com, Lynn O'Shaughnessy, 5/6/2007; the president of Sarah Lawrence College: "The problem is that the U.S. News college rankings are far from reliable." Michele Tolela Myers, *The Cost of Bucking College Rankings,* Washington Post, 3/11/2007; the first of the new generation web-based report cards that allows users to rank universities on the criteria they choose can be found on Canada's Globe and Mail website, http://www.universitynavigator.com. For an "on the ground" perspective of more than 150 colleges, go to 2 websites where students rate their own colleges: www.collegeprowler.com and www.crapcampus.com. Admission blogs, when you can find them, can be very helpful.

Wait-Listed Colleges Accept Wealthier Students Off Waiting Lists, AACRAO

Transcript, www.aacrao.org, Heather Zimar, 5/25/05; *On a college wait-list? It helps to be rich,* S. Silverstein, LA Times, 5/21/05; *For some college hopefuls, wait goes on and on and on,* LA Times website, Larry Gordon, article posted 5/10/2007; *Wait Lists Grow At Some Colleges,* AACRAO Transcript, www.aacrao.org, Heather Zimar, 5/17/2007. NYTimes blog, TheChoice, May 30, 2013.

The 3 Little Pigs Of Financial Aid See tax Form 8863, p. 3. The Katrina

Emergency Tax Relief Act of 2005 increased the Hope Credit to a maximum of $3,000, and the Lifetime Credit to $4,000 for those residents in specified counties of Mississippi and Alabama, and in specific parishes of Louisiana; the proposed legislation, which is The Universal Higher Education and Lifetime Learning Act of 2007, will do the following: simplify and consolidate the 3 tuition tax deductions into one simple, streamlined, and easy-to-understand credit, provides a maximum $3,000 credit that is available on a per student basis, provides a 50% refundable credit that will allow a tax benefit for higher education, is available for all four years of college (public or private), two years of community college, two years of graduate school, and is available to individuals who are updating their skills in a training or certificate program, and the bill expands the type of eligible education expenses that qualify for the tax credit to include room and board, books and

supplies, and transportation. This per year tax credit is calculated by taking 50% of higher education expenses up to $3,000 and then 30% of higher education expenses from $3,000 to $8,000, up to a total maximum lifetime limit of $12,000.

How Students Flunk IN Quote from interview with Patrick M. Callan, on

www.decliningbydegrees.org.

College Money Traps Comments from Peninsula College's newspaper, The

Buccaneer, 2/2/05.

6 Survival Tips Originally *The Seven Survival Skills,* from a press release

printed in a marketing manual, *How to get a million dollars worth of free publicity,* Paul Hartunian, undated."Students typically feel safe around peers, but 80 percent of all crimes on campus are committed by other students. Alison Kiss, program director for Security on Campus, Inc., an advocacy group in King of Prussia, Pennsylvania, says the **first six weeks** of college require special vigilance. Kiss refers to this period as the red zone and says that's when her group sees a 30 percent spike in calls from student victims: "It's when incoming freshmen are most vulnerable to alcohol abuse, hazing and crimes like acquaintance rape. It's the most dangerous period of a student's campus life." From Reader's Digest (www.rd.com), *Is Your College Student Safe At School?*

Why Pay An Expert? www.nasfaa.org. Scroll down and click on "2008-09

Financial Aid Night Material" and scroll down to "Financial Aid Consultants and Scholarship Search Services Fact Sheet," as of 11/11/07.

Ivy League Colleges Wall Street Journal (Online, Sept 13, 2010, Teri Evans

Additional Quote Sources

Book Review by George Leef of *Declining by Degrees: Higher Education at Risk*, Hersh and Merrow edit book that examines higher ed's problems. The John William Pope Center for Higher Education Policy website, 1/25/06; *Grade Inflation: It's Not Just an Issue for the Ivy League*, discussion on the Carnegie Foundation website, R. Terry Ervin's post, 4/22/05 4:36:56 pm; *It's time to give teaching more weight*, Jonathan Zimmerman, Christian Science Monitor website, 3/14/06; *The Cambridge Question*, Mortimer B. Zuckerman, US News & World Report, 4/6/06; *Literacy of College Graduates is in Decline*, Lois Romana, Washington Post, 12/25/05; *Ivory Cower: University presidents have lost their dignity*, Victor Davis Hanson, Wall Street Journal, 8/27/05.

Primary Book Sources

Paying For College Without Going Broke, The Princeton Review, Kalman A. Chany & Geoff Martz, 2005 Edition. Good source for financial aid info, overrated as a primary source.

Paying For College, The Greenes' Guide to Financing Higher Education, Howard R and Matthew W Greene, St Martin's Griffin, 2004. Information on the many legal ways to lower your out-of-pocket costs is markedly absent. Does not meet expectations commensurate with the authors' impressive academic credentials.

How To Go To College Almost For Free, Ben Kaplan, HarperCollins, 2002. The wrong title. It should be, *How You Can Get Into Harvard For Almost Nothing*. If you're applying with similar talents and brains as the author's, this is your Bible.

On Writing the College Application Essay: The Key to Acceptance and the College of your Choice, Harry Bauld, Quill (HarperResource), 1987. Author was an Ivy League admissions director, and this book is witty and instructive.

The New Rules of College Admissions, Edited by Stephen Kramer and Michael London, Fireside Book, 2006. One of the better resources for college admissions with a no-nonsense approach that has encouraging words for the timid and underachieving. Section on financial aid, given the book's title, is inadequate.

The Early Admissions Game, Christopher Avery, Andrew Fairbanks, and Richard Zeckhauser, Harvard University Press, 2004. A bit too academic for the average reader, but informative of the early application process as it relates to elite colleges.

Admission Matters, Sally P. Springer and Marion R. Franck. Jossey-Bass, A Wiley Imprint, 2005. Lots of helpful admission info, but too slanted toward elite school admission. Well formatted and a pleasure to read. Predictably, as with other books whose focus is admissions, the financial aid section isn't very helpful.

1001 Ways to Pay for College, Gen & Kelly Tanabe, SuperCollege, LLC, 2003. Plenty of excellent suggestions, most of which you'll never use. Alarmingly absent is the use of the modified endowment contract as a way to reposition money to qualify for gobs of more aid.

Secondary Book Sources

Declining by Degrees, Richard H. Hersh and John Merrow, Palgrave Macmillan, 2005. An excellent and must-read about higher education getting lower.

Shakespeare, Einstein, and the Bottom Line, David L. Kirp, Harvard Univ Press, 2004. The reality of college as a business is on full display.

The Professors, David Horowitz, Regnery Publishing, Inc., 2006. This author pulls no punches and convinces fairly quickly that too many professors prefer to indoctrinate rather than teach.

Universities in the Marketplace, Derek Bok, Princeton University Press, 2003. A most respected academic, Bok tells it like it is.

The Shadow University, Alan Charles Kors & Harvey Silvergate, HarperPerrenial, 1998. One of the first books to expose the disturbing intellectual culture of the university.

INDEX

Suggested Discussion Questions

1. What is the central idea of the book? What issues does the author explore? Are they personal, economic, political, or sociological?

2. Did the book read like a story, a report, a newspaper article, a diatribe, or something else?

3. One one fact did you learn that stood out the most?

4. What do you feel was the motivation for the writing of this book?

5. What was the point of the book? To explain a topic? Share an opinion? Tell a personal story? Did the author do it well?

6. Do you feel this book belongs in the Education/College nonfiction genre?

7. What part of this book inspired you in some way?

8. Will you read other books by this author?

9. Did this book change your perspective about colleges? In what way?

10. What were the author's major issues?

11. What solutions does the author propose to the problems he raises? Who would implement these solutions? How probable is success?

12. What passages struck you as significant, or interesting, profound, amusing, illuminating, or disturbing? What was memorable?

13. How controversial are the issues raised in this book? Does the author describe them well?

14. What sort of writing style does the author use? Is it objective or subjective? Passionate and earnest? Is it inflammatory or sarcastic? Does the style help or undercut the author's points?

ABOUT THE AUTHOR

Paul Lloyd Hemphill is one of America's leading advocates for revealing the unknown facts that truly benefit students with college admissions and parents with financial aid.

Since he started his college business, he has helped hundreds of families in America send their children to the right-fit colleges without spending their life's savings. Paul was once in the same circumstance as his own clients; he claims to wear the financial scars to prove it.

Paul is a highly sought-after, entertaining speaker and media favorite. He provides insider knowledge on how to get the "edge" in the admissions process by *guiding* students, not coaching them to be someone they're not. Parents also enjoy watching Paul help to legally beat the colleges at their own game of skyrocketing costs.

Paul makes his home in Norfolk, MA with one of God's few but better angels, his wife, Ann Marie. He's a graduate of Assumption College (cum laude) with a double-major in philosophy and theology. He's a decorated Vietnam veteran, having been awarded the Bronze Star Medal and the Vietnamese Cross of Gallantry.

Paul's hobby is writing, editing, and videography. He has produced over 100 videos on college admission and financial aid strategies. His other books, *Why You're Already A Leader* and **Gettysburg Lessons In The Digital Age** are available on Amazon.com.

Before ever knowing of the existence of a FAFSA form, Paul's son John graduated from Salve Regina University; his other son Mark graduated from the University of Massachusetts.

After spending over 25 years in marketing and advertising, he experienced his college mistakes all too painfully, like over-spending by at least $50,000. The content of this book is what he learned *after* the money was spent.